The Marriage Maze...

Shining His Light on the Journey

CHRISTIAN COUPLES' ADVICE FOR A SUCCESSFUL MARRIAGE

JOYCE AKIN

Printed in the United States of America.

ISBN: 978-1-4269-4756-8 (sc)
ISBN: 978-1-4269-4757-5 (hc)
ISBN: 978-1-4269-4758-2 (e)

Library of Congress Control Number: 2010916843

Trafford rev. 11/11/2010

 www.trafford.com

North America & international
toll-free: 1 888 232 4444 (USA & Canada)
phone: 250 383 6864 ✦ fax: 812 355 4082

CONTENTS

WELCOME

Settle in for a Chat

Introduction

This book is intended to help marriages that are newlywed to not-so-new, from a Christian perspective. The advice that you are about to read is from Christian couples across the state of Texas that have experiences in living and producing a solid marriage based on the principles that God has taught them over the years. They are the survivors of making a marriage work and still love each other, which is a rare accomplishment in this day. It has nothing to do with education, economic status or their ethnic background. These folks have a degree in *LIFE* and have graduated with a Masters.

These couples are active in their local church and have been married twenty-five years or more, which is the reason they are in the **'25 PLUS Club'** ......*those are the guidelines that God laid on my heart in writing this book*! My thanks to all the couples that took their time in sharing their pearls of advice; without them I would not have this book. I have lived in Texas all my life and I know the people in this state are from good roots that will tell it like it is.....plain and simple and back to the basics.

You are reading this book because you want to improve or get help for your marriage .There will be a section in each chapter that will be from the **Woman** point of view and **Man** point of view. This will help you to see that we do think differently, but the end result is still to work as One in getting our marriages to work. God made us different so that we would learn to complement each other. We each have different strengths and weaknesses and that is usually what has drawn or attracted us to each other. BUT, these are also the attributes that can be at the foundation of our issues with each other.

They were such attractive traits when you were dating and then they became the very things that were a source of irritation; a source of irritation that has led many to the divorce courts as irreconcilable. Honestly, they probably are irreconcilable, *unless* the Lord is in the center of your marriage and has supernaturally given you the love, understanding and wisdom that you will need to survive .We have all heard about the Mars and Venus personalities that men and women have, and it is true. If you throw out this husband or wife for a newer model, you will be getting another of the same species with a new face, but still basically wired the same. So let's see what we can do to help you understand this odd little creature that you have married. With God's help, you will learn to appreciate your mate and know that there can be a new found love and respect for them. Your marriage will be a maze of twists and turns with ups and downs... the future uncertain. God can help and guide you each step of the way, as He shines His light on your journey.

Find a cozy chair, a cup of coffee and begin to read these pearls of wisdom ….. let's **Settle in for a Chat**.

NEWLYWEDS

NEWLYWEDS

Let the Journey Begin

Chapter One

This first chapter is dedicated to all those young couples about to get married or have been married a short time . Actually, that is how this book came into being. My husband and I were asked to go to an engagement announcement party for a young couple in their early twenties. Toward the end of the dinner, they asked if all the couples would go around and give their advice to them on how to have a successful marriage. I was very impressed at the great advice that the women gave, but *really* impressed with the men's advice. There is just something about when a man speaks and it is good, that it is very good! You know that it is harder for guys to share their feelings, but they did just that. Remember, women can talk ten times more than men, we are just wired that way. So, all that to say, is how this book was originated.

The Lord impressed upon me that there was a need for advice like that for all marriages, because one in two are failing. When a marriage fails, children will suffer, grandparents will suffer, communities will suffer, jobs will suffer and most of all the two people involved will never be the same. Their self-esteem has taken a blow and the real problem is that they are not learning from their mistakes. More often, they are out looking for someone to fill that void, but will repeat the **same** mistakes because they are the **same** people who haven't learned what it takes to make a marriage work. **Same** people, but with more damaged baggage to bring into the next relationship!

There are so many young couples today that have been in several serious relationships before they actually get married, with a high percentage living together first. They think the odds are better of making it if they 'try it out' or 'test drive it' before the actual purchase. I hope that this book will put that theory to rest and prove that *only* with the Lord at the center of your marriage, will there be a realistic chance of making the marriage work. The door swings open easily in a live-in situation to leave if there aren't **serious** commitments behind the vows. That is one of the reasons behind a marriage ceremony, to vow before God and all your loved ones that you are going to make this marriage work and seek Him for help to do that.

Then comes the hard part of actually *doing* it!! I got married at an early age which was fairly common in that day. No, it was not in the horse and buggy days, but in the 60's. Some girls went to college and some got married. That was just the way it was. Today, the popular trend is to get a college education and get that perfect job before getting married. Nothing is wrong with that, but I think that is where so much of the living together comes in to place. It seems all those things have to be perfect and accomplished before you could ever consider settling down with someone. Then, if all that is in place, making a marriage work should happen without too much trouble.

Young couples are puzzled that relationships are such a struggle, but a marriage will take working on everyday. Personalities struggle to have the upper hand and it becomes a tug-of-war of who is going to win this argument or decision. If either of you have come from an indulgent family, that always let you have your way, it is going to be a red flag going in to any relationship. Marriage is about thinking of the other person and what is going to be best for them. If you tend to be selfish or self-centered, the odds of making it with anyone are slim to none, unless there is a change from within that only the Lord can do. If you are thinking of the other person first and their best interest, then you will have an easier time in resolving your conflicts. It will be easier to say "I'm sorry" and to forgive and forget.

I didn't know I could actually pray about a mate and who God wanted for me. I was eighteen and got all my advice from a popular magazine that told me if our personalities were compatible. My test score said we were, so we were! WRONG! I have tried to let people know that test didn't have a clue what it was talking about. We fought for the next ten years over everything. We were a mess! It was during that time that I seriously started seeking God and His word about what makes a person happy and what His scriptures said about marriage.

You can imagine how 'starry-eyed' or naïve I was at eighteen, just graduated from high school and marrying someone twenty-one and on his second marriage, coming in with a small child. The odds of our marriage making it were slim. It has been an incredible adventure that has kept God very busy in doing repair work on two unlikely people who were very opposite in personalities. But, I have learned that most couples are very different and that was our attraction to each other.

Regardless of how old you are as you start this journey with your mate, there will be some bumps, hurdles and mountains to climb to get down the road and achieve the '*25 Plus Club*'. We are a rare group and we want to see all of you make it into this select club that is for everyone who can show courage, endurance, patience, love beyond measure, honesty, loyalty and most of all a walk with God through our Lord Jesus Christ in the power of the Holy Spirit…….*Let the Journey Begin*!

Women's Advice on Newlyweds

Frances Knight:

Understanding the Mars and Venus principle will solve a lot of marriage problems before they get started. In fact, the book, <u>Men are from Mars, Women are from Venus</u> by John Gray should be in every stack of wedding presents. Men and women are different. Not only is he likely to be macho and she more loving and affectionate, they do not think and reason the same. Sometimes it may seem that a spouse's logic is literally from a different planet.

Look at the reasons for some of these misunderstandings: To personalize, think through the sociological differences in your marriage so you can better understand your spouse's mannerisms and views. There are enough contrast to hurdle by just being a man and a woman- without also having radical differences in languages, economic and educational levels, religious convictions and cultural customs with their social graces. These factors make up who you are and who your spouse is.

Always treat your spouse courteously. Remember please, thank you and "Oh, I'm sorry…" Good manners also reflect the right tone of voice, which can soothe . To bring the listener into a receptive mode, shove your volume control lever down:

Megahorn…lecture…preachy… **LOUD** can make the listener feel threatened and defensive. Some people have a loud voice and don't realize how the listener perceives the sound.

Good manners is also to *listen* to his/her views. Too many times we hear, but we don't listen. Listening shows respect for the other person and his/her opinions. It honors them. Then , they will be more receptive to hearing your views. Dialogue is essential.

In the day that I was teaching the Young Married Ladies Bible study, I said, "Make a list of your husband's virtues and the reasons why you married him and keep the list in your Bible." My list is still true today - Bob is handsome, loving, honest, kind, responsible, dependable, generous. Your spouse, too , will tend to be more like what you think and say about him.

Today, after fifty-six years of marriage, our Golden Years are golden because we continue to practice the basic rules for a good marriage and tell each other "I love you" each day.

Patricia Fryling:
As a young bride, I had a lot of expectations. You desire that once you begin your life together, the fun of setting up a household and putting away all the lovely gifts you have received, the magic of life begins. It is so fun and exciting and the making of friends as a couple is so rewarding. Becoming a part of a church where Christ is the focus is so important as it is the lifeline in our Christian walk. When we become part of a church fellowship and help where we can, whether it is teaching, helping in a nursery or becoming involved in our own class of young adults, ministering can be a real blessing and keep us focused on the things that are really important in life. Things that count for Christ are the only things that count in life. Don't let life get too busy; you must talk as a couple to see what your priorities are and move forward on those things.

Mary Ann Martin:
Treat each other with respect. I know we start out very much in love and thrive on each other's presence, but we need to remember to take time for ourselves. Take time in the things of the Lord for yourself.
Serve God first and then each other.

Sandra Dean
'First We Attract, Then We Attack'
- The things that attract us to each other are the same things that will drive us crazy later on in the marriage. New love thinks some things are cute. Old love thinks, "What was I thinking when I married him?"

- Write this down on a note card and review it whenever you contemplate killing him. "He was like this when I married him. What made me think that he would change? Who is the STUPID one here?" Your attitudes and thought life is one of the only things you can change.
- 2 Corinthians 10:5b which states: "..Bringing into captivity every thought to the obedience of Christ."
- Have a structured prayer time at the beginning of each day. That will set the tone for everything else.
- Regularly plan time away and read and discuss a Christian book together.
- Nobody wants to be nagged or to nag, but chores need to be done. Try this: On a chalk board list the things that need to be done with each person submitting their requests. They can perform them on their time schedule. Problem solved, no nagging.

Kay Carol Pemberton:
Communication is a MUST in a new marriage. The couple must share their thoughts and feelings. Marriage is 50/50 and the couple must always remember this. Thoughts and feelings must be shared DAILY! This will lead to a healthy relationship and marriage.

Vicki Clinton:
The honeymoon is over and the most important journey in life begins together. Don't lose sight of the goals that you both want. As newlyweds, write down some goals you want as a couple and individually. You are each other's lover, confidant and best friend. Don't ever take the relationship for granted.

Netta White:
Marriage is a commitment of love to one another to spend the rest of your lives together, not just through the good time, but all the time.

Two people coming together with different upbringing or backgrounds are going to encounter many challenges. The desire to make your marriage work will overcome those challenges.....make each other happy!

Don't Count! Nothing is equal in a marriage. When you start counting all the things you do, and what he doesn't do, you're going to feel resentful and used. Do for him because it makes you feel good and happy…don't expect the same in return or you'll be disappointed. Eventually, over time (patience, patience) he will catch on and reciprocate.

Sylvia Hankin:
First ,always remember that the person you are married to is and should be your best friend, someone you can laugh with , share secrets with, cry with, share embarrassing moments and knowing it will be okay at the end of the day. Your spouse is a blessing from God; always remember that. You don't know when God is going to call either one back home, so don't go to bed upset with each other.

Elma Naranjo:
It is important always to respect your husband and uplift him. Never talk negatively about him or put him down to your friends.…concentrate on his good qualities. I have a wonderful husband who is a great dad that lives his Christianity at home. It blesses me when my children tell me that they have told their friends that we love and respect each other.

Anonymous:
Being married is a relationship; you have to work at it. Sometimes it's hard, other times not so hard. If anyone tells you it's easy, they're lying. Find a church together, even if it's not the one you grew up in. If the church follows Jesus Christ, and you get involved together, it will make it easier for you to follow Him.

Patti Reese:
Be equally yoked. Although you're probably already Christians, where you are in that relationship can range from A-Z. Our core values and non-negotiable Christian principles were in synch with each other and the foundation from which we made decisions.

Maintain a sense of humor. Be able to laugh with one another, not at the other's expense. LAUGH everyday together.

Plan time for just the two of you on a consistent basis. This is harder once the kids start coming in to the family. That can be a date night, movie night, or just a walk through the neighborhood after dinner. This creates the atmosphere for just talking about your day and staying connected on an intimate level.

Be active in your local church serving the Lord. Make it a priority. Using the gifts God has blessed you with, makes you the person God created you to be. This enhances the marriage relationship as well.

We share household responsibilities and chores. We did not have 'that's your job' and 'that's my job', although we gradually shifted in to the areas we naturally were better at or enjoyed doing. He did yard work and I paid bills, as that was what we both enjoyed or were better at doing. Find the balance that makes it work for you…it is a process!

Have a daily quiet time alone with the Lord. Start every day reading God's word so that He can speak to you, comfort , guide , admonish and encourage you. He shows His great love toward us which makes us better able to love others by His design through the power of the Holy Spirit.

Choices…know that all of our choices have consequences, good and bad depending on the ones that we make: words we choose to say , the way we choose to act, the attitude we choose to exhibit. Make the choices you want and can live with.

Make the person you marry your best friend. I still have my *best girlfriends,* but my spouse is my best friend. He who knows me best, loves me the most.

Have outside interests and hobbies apart from your spouse. My husband loves fishing. He loves me best, though, because I never (OK rarely) make him choose between fishing and me.

Phyllis Haas:

Since day one of our marriage, we have always had private devotions together at the breakfast table after the meal…. Bible reading, devotional and discussion. Starting the day off that way is GREAT!

Vicky Abney:

Get married for the right reasons and not until you are mature…ready to put someone else first before your own desires.

Be nice and fun (always). Make your husband feel like he is the most important part of your day.

Tell your husband what you need or want…say it once. Give him time to process /deliver, on his own timing, not always on your timing.

Your appearance, your speech, your moods DO make a difference to your husband. Give it your best shot, everyday.

Tell him every time he does something that really pleases you. Appreciate all his goodness and pray that you won't see his faults.

Stay on your knees in prayer, asking God to give you wisdom and love for others.

Mary Anne Betancourt:
You need to respect your husband. We live in an age of man bashing, making fun of husbands. But that is not what the Word of God says. Wives are to respect their husbands. Women tend to think love is as important to men as it is to them, but surveys show men value and need respect more than even love.

If I ask the Lord to help me set my heart in obedience to His Word and show me how to respect my husband, He will honor that request. One obedience produces another: as I respect him, the love I so need from my husband grows – and we reflect the Word of God!

Jodie Stryker:
This advice was given to me by the smartest woman I know, my mother. Whenever a couple has a disagreement or argument, don't tell your parents. It changes how they see the other person and when you have kissed and made up, they are still upset with them.

Debbie Morris:
Supporting your spouse in career choices can be difficult, if the career does not seem profitable, is time consuming or seemingly a dead-end. Maybe you feel your spouse is not reaching their full potential. Talk it over and understand your spouse's reasoning for making the choice and support them in any endeavor. Pray about the career direction you should each be taking.

Barbara Sullivan:

Let God pick your mate and agree with His selection

Pray for your husband-pray scripture with his name in it and ask God to reveal areas that need encouragement or rebuking. God often speaks when we are quiet or in the middle of the night .He may wake you to pray, so ask Him what to pray about.(Psalm 1)

Do not speak downgrading about him. Make note of his positive points such as looks, work successes, leadership of home, fathering, sense of humor, insights, accomplishments, especially with children listening.

If for some reason you must lead the family because of health, military leave, or work issues...ask God for guidance and direction. Hopefully, when he returns to leadership, you can easily let go of control because of walking in submission to God.

Men's Advice on Newlyweds

J.B Morris:
If you want to have a lasting and meaningful relationship with your spouse that can stand the test of time, don't live separate lives! Find things together that you both enjoy, and do them as a couple. It may not be particularly interesting doing something that your mate wants, but you are interested in your mate! Who knows! You may really enjoy yourself. Make one of the activities you pursue as a couple is to be involved in a local church!

Larry Pemberton:
God first! Couples cannot survive without putting God first in their relationship. A daily walk with God is the only way marriages can survive in today's world.

Ron White:
You married each other because you loved each other, right?
Then don't try to change your mate! With time, you will both know what causes your arguments or fights- stay away from those sensitive areas. The right time will present itself to approach those issues.

Harry Reese:
The Biblical command for husbands to *love* their wives and wives to *respect* their husbands as head of the family is given out of the most basic need of the other person.

Spend intimate time getting to know each other. Relationships are cultivated like a garden...the loving, caring and nurturing that goes into it produces a bountiful harvest.

Laurel Haas:

Always remember to put God first in your lives, family and then others. There is NO other way to do it.

It seems the trend now is to live together and then decide to get married or not. That is NOT what the Bible says. You need a true commitment from the start.

There will be ups and downs in life. As we were being counseled before our marriage, the pastor said Ephesians 4:26 and we have tried to follow that all our lives: "Be ye angry and sin not; let not the sun go down upon your wrath."

Talk it out and don't let little things become HUGE mountains.

Terry D. Hankin:

You need to realize that marriage is a union between a man and a woman as one. There is no beginning and no end in a ring, so should your commitment be to each other as well. There are no breaks in a ring, so there should not be any breaks in your marriage to each other. And let us not forget that God should always be there in the center of it.

Fred Akin:

Have fun and get to know each other. Don't take yourselves and each other too seriously.....life will get serious quick enough.

Don't rush into having children...wait several years to get stability in your marriage.

If you have an argument, don't call your mom and dad...work your problems out!

Get involved in church.

Adrian Fryling:

Marriage is a melding together of two individual lives who have been raised differently. To be successful, these individuals must be modified and rearranged to operate as one individual. Love for one another, a dedication to the wellbeing of the other and a willingness to forego individual preferences for the sake of a successful outcome. The building of a new relationship of this magnitude requires maturity and a depth of love that is more than a physical attraction. This depth of love motivates us to give our everything for the purpose of strengthening the union and supporting our mate. This will help us to share our burdens and face challenges.

Encouragement and support is the daily goal....avoid being critical. Supporting one another in deep love will help to keep away discouragement and depression.

Work together to keep a clean and organized home. That shows you care and it will present an image of who you are.

Eat meals together and help with the planning of meals. Contribute with preparation of the meals. Set the table and help clean up after. Working on this together can build a bond of love.

Commit to be faithful to your mate and resisting any other attraction that would steal the love you have for each other. Pray together and present your needs and concerns to God. Pray for your mate that God will develop in them to be an example of His indwelling love.

Always ask the Lord to guide you in your walk and He will show you the way. I always say that a marriage is like a beautiful garden. It takes a lot of work, keep it watered, nurture it and it will grow. Keep the weeds out. This takes time but must be done as they can creep in unnoticed at times. Always give your garden the love it requires.

Louis Ikerd:
True love loves unconditionally. It is a 100% commitment by both spouses. True love is tempered by faithfulness, forgiveness, and a willingness to work together in good times and bad. A marriage anchored on the foundation of Jesus Christ will stand the test of time. Never, ever, let pride interfere with saying: " I am sorry, please forgive me" or " I love you."

Mike Sullivan:
First, even before marriage, be sure that there are not a large number of differences between you. Race differences can cause serious problems due to differing customs. Drinking and smoking –if partner does and the other doesn't- can be another cause for problems and failure. Differences

in religion or being unequally yoked(believer and unbeliever) will prove to be a challenge for any marriage. Having Jesus at the center of your life is a glue that holds you together through thick and thin.

Duane Stryker:

Husbands never tell your wives that this is not how your mother did something (not how mom makes her potato salad, etc.) This does not sit well with your spouse and can cause tension between the two most important women in your life – your wife and your mother.

Louis Martin:

Not many people at an early time in their marriage think of the Lord. There is so much more to do!!! I didn't, even though I was raised in a Christian home. Try to keep Jesus as the head of your house. The old saying is true of " Families that worship together, stay together."

Ralph Cochran:

We give each other compliments and say how blessed we are to have each other . In the morning, we watch Christian TV , read the Bible together and pray. This starts a wonderful day and I know has made us so thankful for everything God has given us – especially each other, children and grandchildren. We are thankful for a wonderful church family and having a pastor that is <u>real</u>*!*

Bob Knight:

> Love your wife with all your heart.
> Be honest, dependable, and faithful to her.
> Respect your wife and express confidence in her decisions.
> Work diligently.
> Seek God's opinion…pray.
> Never have separate rooms.
> "Drop it" when there are unresolved differences of opinion.
> Keep up repairs around the house – and plant flowers.

ARGUMENTS

ARGUMENTS

Slam-Bam....I'm Gone!

Chapter 2

The remainder of this book is intended to cover the topics that are some of the biggest problems that most marriages will face. I can tell you that in forty-five years of marriage, we have had some humongous, hum-dinger, over–the-top arguments!! I mean like "Who is going to pack and leave … me or you?" for the 100th time!! Our suitcases just stayed out since we knew we would have another argument over something that we couldn't agree on. It really took us a long time to learn to *discuss* and be friends.

We should have gone to get some counseling and learned to fight nicely, but we didn't. I suggested it many times, but that meant you would have to talk to a stranger about your personal problems and lay it all out there. Well, you can just imagine that my introvert, quiet and private husband really loved that idea. He was raised that you don't air the dirty laundry with anyone…that just wasn't right. It was un-American to him. On the other hand, I was raised with three sisters that talked about everything, spoke our peace and cleared the air. Again, it's that opposite- attract- thing, was in every aspect of our lives.

When you spoke your peace, it was easy to move on since the air was now cleared. But if you tend to be the private, quiet type, then you simmer and simmer until there is an explosion. I would think that everything was fine until some little something would happen and all of a sudden, he was gone for awhile….sometimes a long while!

We were so young and these were the kind of things that showed a real immaturity. I see some similarities in the couples getting married today, although most are not too young, but they do seem to be somewhat self-centered and immature since they have been doing their own thing for a long time. The divorce rate is at an all time high, so there is room for improvement about how to *agree to disagree*.

Let's talk about the 'tone of your voice' problem. This can make all the difference in how your mate is going to accept or reject your opinion on a subject. Ladies, if you would please do as I say and not as I did. I would get all worked up and be in a frenzy by the time we got together to discuss the issue. He would be walking in the door after a long day at work and I would just blurt out exactly how I felt. Needless to say, he would be totally blind-sided. His first defense was to shut down and not hear anything that was being said. This would end up with him storming off to the bedroom and slamming the door in my face. I had a LOT to learn about this clearing- the- air method I had learned growing up.

As I began to mature in the Lord, this was one area that my husband said he could see a big difference in me. That difference was that I started **praying** about what I was upset about and asked God to give me wisdom on how to say it in a right and loving way that would not hurt his ego and pride. When a man's ego and pride has been shredded by his wife, it will take a long time to rebuild. It can be a dangerous time in a marriage. I do think that this can be an underlying reason for a lot of affairs that get started. 'Other' women can sense in a man when things are not going well at home and they have had their eye on this fine catch for awhile…. sad but true!

There is a verse that says "Satan has come to steal, kill and destroy" John 10:10. Satan wants marriages destroyed because they are the foundation of our society, so he is out there stirring up trouble every minute that he can. When there is a crack in that ego, that God instilled in a man, then there will be danger lurking. We faced some of these problems and I had to really take a long look at myself and take a lot of blame for how I was handling discussing problems.

Back to learning to pray before speaking , this was a process. Don't give up if you blow it, but keep getting before the Lord and asking him to show you a better way to discuss. Be creative on how to approach an issue. My husband would always be shocked if I said I was sorry shortly after an argument. Sometimes there would be a **week** go by that we did not say a word to each other. Although this was probably a joy to him, it was excruciating to me and a tenseness was in the air. Our poor kids got to see this fine behavior for many years. Thank you God that they didn't turn out damaged over this, but good decent human beings. They knew we loved each other, but had a strange way of showing it.

My goal was to see if I could lovingly get Fred to open up and share what he was feeling about a problem. I would rehearse different ways of how to say something to him…this might go on for several days before a right time to actually talk to him. I learned he is a morning person, so usually at night was too late to discuss the big issues. He would overreact because he was tired and the outcome was usually not good. I also learned that it was better to take it in little increments at a time, so that each part could be digested before going to the next part. For instance, a nice ride to the beach allowed us time to talk a little at a time since the ride was at least an hour and I knew he was driving and couldn't escape by jumping out. In other words, he was a captive audience and was willing to listen if I just took my time in presenting it. Also, his attitude and frame of mind was good since we were taking a relaxing and fun drive for an evening out to stroll on the beach and just enjoy the fresh air and each other…on a date.

May I say it again, the tone was still an overriding factor that I had to learn to keep in a calm voice. There are still times that it gets the better of me, but God has really done a work in my life in that area.

I am a passionate person and when I get on a soap box about something, then I will do everything in my power to get you to understand and feel the same way. When I became a Christian, I was sure Fred would want to do the same. I had the most amazing change in my life and the person of Jesus Christ loved me unconditionally… WOW!! Well, who wouldn't want to become a Christian?? Not Fred! He thought I had joined some kind of religious cult and he was not going to have any part of it.

We began arguing about church and any topic that was concerned with it. I probably kept him away from church for years by not letting him *see* the change in me versus me *talking* him to death about every newfound revelation that I had come across.

Several years later he did become a Christian, due in large part to our kids asking him to come to church like all the other Dads. Amazing how God works through the sweetness of a child. I do remember him asking me if I had gotten the kids to ask him to come to church, and I honestly could say that God got them to do that without my help. Of course, I had to get out of God's way so that He could patiently get his attention about His love. God made it very clear to me that He was going to use me to *show* him love unconditional and use other people to *talk* to him about His love.

Scriptures tell us," Wives …be submissive to your husbands, so that , if any of them do not believe the Word, they may be won over without words by the behavior of their wives, when they see the purity and reverence of your lives. Your beauty should not come from outward adornment… Instead, it should be that of your inner self, the unfading beauty of a gentle and quiet spirit, which is of great worth in God's sight."(1 Peter 3:1-4) That was a foreign idea to me since I love to talk, but then God has His own way of doing things that are not our ways. Then He can take total credit for the change. Now you are beginning to see that this is a process. It takes a walk with Him on a daily basis, as your marriage is a daily event that is continually changing before your eyes.

The story of Esther really caught my attention in the way she chose to discuss important subjects. Her people were about to be annihilated and she had to go before her husband, the king. This was going to be tricky as she had not been invited to come before him. She had her people praying and fasting that she would have favor to talk to him and get this stopped. Read this wonderful book and see how she took her time and asked him in stages to be assured that this destruction of her people would not happen. God went before her because she prayed for wisdom and timing in how to present this urgent issue. She also stayed calm and lovingly set the stage that was conducive for him to hear her request.

Husbands, it would be wise to understand that women are very complex human beings and we are made up of many parts.…physically and mentally. Pay special attention when it is that time-of- the-month approaching, as we will react oddly to problems that usually don't upset us. It is smart to avoid serious conversations at this time and tread lightly. It will pass in a few days and all we need is some TLC from you and don't take us too seriously at this time. When hormones are out of whack, so are we! Of course, this can also take into account when Moms are expecting.…. this can be nine months of treading lightly, but that can be the price for that little bundle of joy. Please encourage your little sweetie to go get those annual exams and make sure some of the 'hardware' has not gotten out of kilter. Doctors used to not pay attention to those mood swings after birth, but now they take it very seriously.

Children being raised in today's society will all be taught the 'Time-Out' method. We as adults can learn from this. When an argument starts getting heated and out of control....STOP! Go to another part of the house or go sit outside and cool down. We need to get out of each others presence and really think about what has been said. There can be some merit in what your mate is trying to tell you, but it may be coming out all wrong or hurtfully said. This is when you **don't** need to get in a car and drive away in anger. Too bad our cars aren't electronically geared to shut down because they know you are in a state of anger and could potentially be a threat on the road.

Call in the Troops! When there is a big argument, women want to call every friend, sister and mother to tell them how terrible their husband has just treated them. Actually, they are getting our side of the story , so we will feel justified for being so upset and feeling so mistreated. It is a really good friend, sister or mother that will pray with you and be honest, that just maybe, you are over- reacting and that there is some truth in what has been said. In time we usually cool down and makeup, but all the friends are still waging a war over this jerk you have married.

The more we understand what makes each other tick, then we can better understand how and when to wisely approach topics for discussion. If you can learn from our mistakes, you will be able to avoid: ***Slam-Bam.....I'm Gone!***

Women's Advice on Arguments

Sandra Dean:
Absolutely no name calling. Don't start a sentence with "You always…..".

Write down your thoughts after you have had a chance to cool down and explain things in a way that he can understand. One way is to tell a story about a facetious person and describe how she felt. That can defuse an argument and help both parties understand where the other is coming from.

Netta White:
Does it really matter who wins the argument? If you have to give in sometimes to keep peace in the family- do it! It is not going to make you less of a woman. If you're right , your spouse will know it.

He will try to make it up to you in other ways. Sometimes, he'll even admit to being wrong….but then he may not!

Sylvia Hankin:
Don't let every one know your business. Talk and discuss in another room if there is someone else in the house. Don't let it get out of hand, but try to solve it and make-up. Pray and ask God for advice. Remember that God does not remember what happened the day before, so try to do the same.

Phyllis Haas:
Again talk it out, don't let little things fester. Pray the Lord can show YOU how to help the situation.

Vicky Abney:
Listen to what your husband has to say, as he is probably making a pretty good point. Always try to put yourself in his shoes to see if you can understand where he is coming from. We have never argued much because we both respect and try to honor the other. It's not a brag, just a learned communication skill. Never criticize your mate in front of others.

Barbara Sullivan:
Like the referee says in a boxing match: No low blows! Learn to fight nicely – easier said than done. When fighting – resist the urge to win and always have the last word in victory. You really don't win if you win a battle and lose a war (ie, win a fight and lose a marriage).

When you are having troubles, do your best to stay in the same house (especially for the security of the children). Do not speak of leaving unless abused or fear of it.

Try not to go to bed fighting, but if you do, then pray for your partner. Remember that God can speak to the other's heart and present your case (He is your advocate/lawyer.)

After fighting, really try to be quiet as it provides cool down time. When criticized – agree if it is true and if you don't know ask God to reveal the truth in their words. If it is an area of correction, ask your spouse to pray for you. When a marriage is really having a rough time, it is showing that the couple are extreme opposites and God needs to bring them into balance.

Gold Nugget: God is correcting and perfecting you to be the bride of Christ through your spouse. A divorce means that another person will have to be used by God to be the piece of iron that sharpens iron. There will be conflict with whoever you are married to.

If you choose to take the lead in your marriage, you'll probably miss the husband's covering/protection. Satan can have more influence for destruction of the family (I cite Eve as an example).

Mary Ann Martin:
It has been said by many not to go to bed mad, but, there are times when my husband and I have decided to do just that. We rarely even argue. We may go to bed not speaking and as the next day goes on, one of us will call the other and apologize or hug in the kitchen, while getting dinner ready. Of course, you shouldn't let silence go on for long. I'm just telling what has worked for us. And don't try and bring up the old stuff. As my grandmother used to say "let it lye."

Patti Reese:
- Try to realize when an argument is escalating. Take a break and let things cool down. This seems to be harder for women to do than men.
- Fight Fair. Keep to the issue at hand. DO NOT bring up unresolved or past issues.
- Choose what you say so that you have no regrets or destroy the trust between you.
- We did not always argue in 'private'. We wanted our kids to know that we did not always agree on everything (or even appear to). We wanted them to know that arguing does not mean divorce or that we did not love each other any more. They knew it was safe to have a difference of opinion and to express it appropriately.

Vicki Clinton:
Focus on what the disagreement is about and what needs to be resolved. Maybe it's as simple as, whether or not to let your child go spend the night with a friend. Mom says no, Dad says yes. There is not a right or wrong answer and in these instances, I would let the husband make the final decision. In the home, God has put the husband as the head and the protective umbrella over the family. Pray about it and God will lead.

Kay Carol Pemberton:
Never go to bed angry. This is so difficult, but it is a practice that every couple should adhere to. Talk out the problems and what causes the anger.

Frances Knight:

Bob and I have had a good marriage and we aren't experts on the subject of arguing. So, some of my suggestions are from common sense and some are from experience. Common sense says,

"**Never, never, never**, yell, slam doors, throw things, shove, touch your spouse in a threatening way, or screech tires and head for the unknown."

Now this is from experience- "**Hold your tongue**". Don't spout off everything that pops into your mind. Words can inspire, encourage and motivate. Or, when used as weapons, they can destroy self-esteem, a marriage – and even a life. Remember, words can never be retrieved.

A good thing to do when the conversation is getting out of hand is breathe deeply three times and slowly count to four hundred thirty-seven (Read James 3:1 – 12 about Taming the Tongue).

"**Do not let the sun go down while you are still angry**, and do not give the devil a foothold (Eph. 4:26-27)." That means forgive and do it before bedtime. After it is dark and you are lying in bed thinking, it is easy to meditate on the negatives until everything is blown out of proportion. In that mood, the devil has a wide open door to inspire you to call your lawyer *first thing in the morning* – over something you may not even remember by next Thursday.

What to do after a heated discussion: A marriage is blessed when there isn't enough money to hop on a plane and zoom off to Florida. It is cheaper to just walk around the block. Early in our marriage, my husband and I agreed to never even sleep in separate rooms when we are at odds with each other. As a result, there is not much distance between each other when you are in the same bed...what a thrill, when shortly before dawn, you sense a foot reaching over to touch yours. It can't happen if you are in *another room – in Florida.*

Apologize and admit it when you are wrong. "I'm sorry, I made a wrong decision...wrong judgment...acted unwisely...jumped to conclusions... didn't think it through, or I didn't have enough information." "Really, it was a stupid thing that I did and I am truly sorry – Please forgive me." Did you notice that the above statements are a judgment against wrong decisions – not the condemnation of a person. **Never** degrade your husband/wife as a person – (i.e., "You are a failure.") Speak only of issues.

Anonymous:

Keep on topic. Don't yell; don't threaten; don't curse. Listen to the other point of view. Ask yourself "Is this really important? Will it make a difference 5 years from now?" Sometimes you have to agree to disagree. When it's over, it's over. Proverbs 21:19 "It is better to dwell in the wilderness, than with a contentious and angry woman."

Men's Advice on Arguments

Harry Reese:
You will not agree on everything all the time and when that happens;
Remember: Listen to what they say;
   Listen for what they do not say;
   Conflict can be positive to get a viewpoint you never perceived.
   Hearing is a function; Listening is a skill
   You are help-mates to each other.
Reminder: Biblical command : Do not let the sun go down and still be angry ; make-up and kiss good-night!

Louis Martin:
Everyone has arguments which is human nature. My wife and I have never had an argument in front of our children that I can remember. You need to keep this between you and your wife and in private. But believe me we have had arguments.

Larry Pemberton:
Men tend to not understand why wives are angry with them. Wives seem to just shut down. We must try to get our wives to open up and express their feelings so we understand what is wrong and make the necessary changes.

Fred Akin:
Arguments start out small and seem to escalate into World War 3. There seems to never be a 'winner' in these situations, so my advice is to learn to 'bite your tongue'. Get some space from your spouse, until you can talk about it calmly and lovingly. Take a break and calm down!!

Louis Ikerd:
Be willing to listen and be very careful in the words you choose as a reply or rebuttal. Use self control and gentleness in the process of working through such arguments. Sometimes it is best to wait until the next day to work out a solution to your disagreements. I quote my granddaughter "build a bridge and get over it."

Dempsie Clinton:
Arguments are going to happen. Just grin and bear it, I mean bury it, as fast as possible. You don't have to win every battle, just win the war

Terry D Hankin:
Never allow yourselves to call each other names as you reason with each other. Talk things over and try to come to an understanding without raised voices or tempers. Understand each others wants and needs and compromise. Don't air out disagreements in public, but discuss it openly with each other in private.

Jaime Naranjo:
- We argue like all marriages do.
- Before our arguments get heated, we walk away from each other to cool off. It works.
- We say we are sorry to each other and don't discuss it anymore. But she (wife) is usually right.
- Then we ask the Lord to take over our problem.
- We never argue in front of our kids.

Mike Sullivan:

Arguments are inevitable; however, when we remember that we are one, to argue with our mate is to argue with our self. At the very least, if we want to be successful in our marriage, we need to control our emotion. We have a tendency to say things we don't really mean, but once the words come out of our mouth we cannot grab them and put them back. Those words have barbs that not only bring pain, but stick and are remembered for some time. Be angry and sin not.

Ron White:

Sometimes, it's better to walk away from an argument before it progresses to the point of no return. When you lose your temper – you lose! Getting away for a little while might give you a better perspective of the situation. Don't go to bed angry! The longer you carry anger, the more it festers. Sometimes, all it takes is a little kind gesture from you to make things "okay." You love each other!

FINANCES

FINANCES

"Where did it all go?"

Chapter 3

We got married at a young age and there was little to prepare us for handling finances. It was paycheck to paycheck and struggle to struggle. Neither of us had a degree, so we made it on minimum wage with children quickly entering into our lives. I can remember when our first child was due and we had no insurance, I asked if they were going to keep the baby until we could pay our hospital bill. The nurse promptly asked me to go to the accounting office and set up payments. That was our first pay-it-out experience!

As we got promotions in our jobs and began to make more money, of course, we spent more. When you start off early having children, you quickly realize that money is going out at record speed. As time marched on , credit cards began to be very accessible, which gave us a lot of freedom to have all those things that we wanted…...nicer home, better car, vacations, clothes, jewelry. Everyone else had those things and so should we! I don't think the mind-set is too different today than it was 30-40 years ago….we work hard and we deserve to have what we want! Credit cards just helped us to get it faster and for a small and affordable payment each month. It was so much fun getting and buying all those things.

It took a while for reality to set in. As jobs changed and salaries changed…no problem! We continued with our same lifestyle , since we could charge it and live very comfortably. After several years of that, it was quite apparent that we were heading for a fall off the cliff. I will never forget watching an Oprah show where she said that 75% of Americans were in serious debt. That caught my attention…..we were in the same situation they were. Couples with $50,000 -$100,00 plus of accrued debt and a looming divorce was facing most of them. All were living in very nice homes and had the nicest that life could afford. In some cases, the husband or wife was clueless that the other spouse had been charging all the cards to maximum and also opening up new cards (the credit card people are so accommodating).

I watched this program for 6 weeks and began to realize I was no different than they were, just on a smaller scale. I had better get serious about getting this turned around and quickly. I also started watching Suze Orman and Dave Ramsey to get their advice. I wasn't going to get a financial advisor to live in our home for a month like all the couples on Oprah, so I knew I better do the next best thing and get help from books and internet financial advisors. First of all, I had to tell my husband that I was concerned about our finances. I was paying the bills, so he just spent until I told him not to. I should have been showing him our income against our debts. That was my first mistake….taking it all on my shoulders and not bringing him in to the total picture of what was happening.

Let's be honest here… I was not wanting to tell myself that life was about to change and we were going to have limits on what we could do. That was not going to be 'fun', so I put it off. By the time I had told him what shape our finances were in, he was in unbelief. He knew that he had some major setbacks with job and salary changes, but I had juggled all of it so well that couldn't we continue to do so?? Being honest can be so painful….with each other and yourself. This was going to require a big change, which was to sell our home and pay off our debts. Actually, I remember waking up one morning after the 6 weeks of debt programs and I knew the Lord very clearly spoke to my heart and said "Sell your home!" Oh boy, that was not what I wanted to hear Him say to me. How in the world was I going to tell Fred that wonderful news?? With time, he came to see that as a solution also. We got a debit card after paying off the credit cards so that we would always know exactly where we were in our finances. We also made an agreement that I would keep him informed of where our money was being spent.

I really think it is good for the husband to be in charge of paying and managing the bills, but it is not wrong for the wife to do that if she is better at math and managing money. Regardless of who is doing it, you have a responsibility to the other to communicate month to month how things are going. This also allows the other person, that if they have to take over the bills due to an illness, absence or death, that they are ready to step in and get the job done. Purchases should always be discussed and agreed on *before* buying. This process of discussing first will bring about a bond that you are both working as a team toward goals that you have agreed on beforehand. It also shows honor to each other about their opinion and worth as a vital part of being a family. A *big* purchase should cause you to pray together and ask God if it is His will before taking that step. If you aren't being given the time to take a few days to pray about a big purchase, then you are probably going into the decision too quickly and may have some later regrets that you had not waited on God to bless the decision.

I am a little amazed at the number of couples in the younger generation that have separate bank accounts....His and Her Money! I know that this stems from later marriages, but it seems to defeat the 'We' in working as a team and learning to consider each others opinion about all purchases. This is good for your children to see this process, as they also know you are a united front about their buying decisions.

There are some differing opinions about children getting allowances, but I think it is good for them so they can start learning to manage money at an early age. They are working for it just as you have to do everyday. My daughter completely changed her buying habits when I sent her to do shopping for the new school year. I gave her a set amount to spend as she wished, but that was going to be it for the fall semester for clothes. She looked for bargains and made the money stretch as far as it could. Before that, she would go with her Dad and beg for all the name brands that sent the cost soaring. There are work programs at school, which let them earn their own money. The benefits are priceless about earning a living and giving them an appreciation for what you do on a daily basis to provide a roof over their head.

Open up a savings account and also teach them the value of tithing back to the Lord, honoring Him that provides the work and health to do it. That is what I would do if I had it to do over...so learn from my mistakes. You will be amazed to know that our adult children are very good money managers and have invested wisely. We are so proud of them, knowing that it was certainly not learned from us. There is much more of a trend today to *not* be in debt and all kinds of programs out there to help you get out.

We have recently seen the housing market in a downward spiral with foreclosures. This was largely due to an earlier government program that allowed people to buy a home at a low interest rate that would escalate over time. That, plus a recession with a lot of job losses, had America looking closely at spending patterns and tightening their belts as they never had before. It was a good thing, because families were getting back to some basics of living on what you make and not on charge cards. America is the 'land of plenty' and we have certainly lived up to our name. One thing we have learned as a country is that we won't die if we cut back. Lets keep in mind that all this spending goes back to **pride**….I will get the best for my family, no matter what the cost is. You are not a failure if you are not buying all that you want. You are showing wisdom and patience to save toward a possession and get it as your money allows or don't get it at all. Somewhere along the way, it became important to have it all. Our parents didn't have it all and they were fine. It just seems each future generation wants to step it up a notch from how they were raised or we are *not successful*. That is a lie straight from the depths of hell…Satan is out to steal, kill and destroy. It is just another way to rob families of their joy by being in debt and will cause many to get a divorce.

Husbands and wives are getting so caught up in the next promotion so we can have more '*stuff*', that we are leaving quality time with our families in last place. When it is all said and done and life is over, what are your children going to say about you as a father or mother…."They worked all the time" or "They were the best parents you could have and were there to support me in all that I did." That, my friend, is the bottom line of being a *success* in life as a parent and it is a constant struggle to get a balance in that area.

A rule of thumb by most financial counselors is to have at least 3-6 months or more of savings put aside for an emergency…we did not get that memo when we got married! Our savings was a piggy bank and it was usually depleted by everyday emergencies. My suggestion is to get something taken out of your check and put away (savings, 401k, CD, etc.) where it is hard to get a hold of it. Life will always have its emergencies and most of us are not well prepared for it.

We have a life insurance policy which is in place to protect our home and bills if one of us were to die. We also made up a will, since we own a home , which is imperative to do this for the remaining spouse and children. We also did a living will , in case one of us got sick and was being kept alive by machines. Take advantage of any health insurance you can possibly afford. You may think that all this is overkill on wills and insurance , but life can bring some unexpected left turns and it is better to be prepared for these unwelcome events. The stories of those that didn't prepare are very sad and are usually what prompts others to get these things done. A lot of wills can be done from internet sites and are free or your bank may have some general ones that will protect your property and children. If both of you are going on a trip by plane, please consider these options before going.

Unfortunately, the health insurance and life insurance will put a dent in the monthly expenses and are optional. BUT, the alternative of not having it leaves you unprotected where you can ultimately lose everything that you have worked to achieve....better safe than sorry!!!

From a Christian perspective, scriptures tell us of the importance of tithing. You may be saying, I have too much going out as it is, now you are asking me to consider tithing. This is really foundational in a Christian's life. Let me share why I feel it is important. When I became a Christian, I turned over my life to the Creator of my soul and all that was important to me. I wanted Him to now be the One that I looked to for all my needs (Jehovah Jireh) and direction in life. This was to include my pocketbook.... ouch!!!!

You can really go through some tough arguments with yourself why there just isn't enough left to also give to church. Why in the world would God ask us to give money back to Him that owns the world..... does He need my money? No, He doesn't need your money, but He does need your obedience and your stewardship of all He has given to you. Tithing is just another way of showing ***honor*** and saying "thank you" for providing me with a job and the health to get up and go to work each day. Teach your children from an early age this principle and they will grow to be wise adults about their money and spending habits. Tithing also keeps the doors open to your local church and the staff needed to operate it. Most importantly, it allows money for missions and ministries in the community that helps families in need to hear about Jesus Christ , His love and what He has done for them....the ***GOSPEL MESSAGE***!

Financial challenges are going to come your way sooner or later, but it will be easier if you can take these suggestions and apply them to your life, marriage and family. Following these principles will hopefully keep you from asking: ***"Where did it all go???"***

Women's Advice on Finances

Vicki Clinton:

Finances have a huge impact on your life. Be open with each other. If you buy something don't hide it. If you got a bonus, don't hide it. You should go over your finances together, at least once a month. Set goals for savings for something special: vacations, furniture. Achieving goals together is very rewarding. If one spouse if spending too much and the other one is worrying how to pay for it, it can put a heavy burden on the marriage.

Gladys Myers:

Don and I have always been a team. We were giving 10% to our church when we married. I have always worked and we raised one son. When our house loan was paid off, we started giving 20%, as I firmly believe you cannot out give God!! I paid all the bills and made sure the bills did not exceed our income by making a list each month of estimated bills versus income. Start a savings account.

Lea Cochran:

We have never had our finances under separate names. Everything is in both our names. We tithe, and he gives us more than we give. Major financial decisions have been made by both of us after we pray about it.

Anonymous:

Talk, talk, talk. Usually one person is better at paying bills and keeping track; you have to recognize that person. I am not an advocate of separate accounts. Give your first 10% to God , put another 10% in your savings. Don't go into debt; especially credit card debt. With the exception of your home and car, pay cash for everything.

Patti Reese:

We always had one checking account. It was our money (we both work outside the home), so we always had conversations about how we spent our money…tithing, savings, investing, etc. We really discussed what we could afford, how we used credit cards (for our convenience -not to create a lifestyle we could not afford). This goes back to discussing core values.

Sandra Dean:

Ladies, realize that when you spend more money than you should, that you are putting your husband under increased stress and therefore stressing your marriage. Is that new outfit really worth it? 1 Peter 3: 3-4.

Get out of debt as soon as possible and stay that way. It frees you up to enjoy your life. When you are in debt you may have to stay in a job that you hate. Proverbs 22:7.

Pat Fryling:

Finances are a vital concern for couples as it can make or break you. Make sure all major purchases are talked about and then prayed for as what may be the right decision. All decisions should be made together, otherwise it can be a thorn in one's side and it is easy to blame the other person if it fails. If it does fail and you are in it together, it is easier to go through it and learn from your mistakes. Making mistakes doesn't mean you're a failure, but once the blame sets in, it can easily snowball into larger things. Don't let it happen to you. Take the responsibility and go on with life and learn from your mistakes. Sometimes when you wait, something better comes along, as we always say, "It's a God thing."

Sylvia Hankin:
Remember to tithe and also save some money. Don't be foolish and try to get every credit card that is offered to you. It is very easy to overcharge, and hard to repay if the finances are tight. Make spending decisions together. Pray for each other that God gives you wisdom with your finances.

Barbara Sullivan:
Finances are a slippery slope – hopefully the husband realizes his responsibility to be the head of the home. However, sometimes a wife is a better leader in this area. If so, she may need to be extremely careful to keep him fully aware of financial situations. This can bring them into a parent (wife) – child (husband) relationship where he turns over his paycheck and then spends it carelessly and extravagantly. He is expecting her to make ends meet because he gave her all his money, "so he has to charge his expenses."

Debbie Morris:
If you're like most married couples this will be the greatest source of stress in your marriage. The best thing you can do is discuss your beliefs about money before you get married. Keep an open line of communication where money is concerned. Work toward the same goals. Live on less! Build a savings! Be honest to each other.

Frances Knight:
Through 57 years of marriage, Bob and I have believed that we are one. He has always insisted that we share equally in everything. He has been a responsible financial manager-even through the years when we had little to manage.

When young couples have to struggle financially, it is not all bad. Many times it causes them to reevaluate their capabilities and hidden talents. New ideas for businesses and innovations can emerge. I started a sewing school for teens that was a grand success for seventeen years. Hundreds of young women learned to design their wardrobes; they made quality dresses , gowns, suits and coats. We had many style shows. For me, and for them, creativity was fun and rewarding.

Bob believes in "pay as you go"; if you don't pay , don't go. Live within your means and don't even try to keep up with those who can afford more.

Be happy with your standard of living. Don't even consider owning the biggest house on this side of town or the latest model auto, if you can't afford it. That way, you can sleep at night.

Agree on large purchases. I remember one time we agreed on a large recliner-for-two at the Texas State Fair. We were so tired and that chair felt so wonderful. Besides, we justified the expenditure by envisioning cozy evenings watching television. When the luxurious chair arrived- *we settled in*. One problem: The payment didn't settle into our small budget. With the price tag still dangling, we packed it up and sent it back. What a relief when it was gone! I am glad there were no credit cards in those days.

Being responsible with finances builds trust in a marriage. Bob gave me an Unlimited Power of Attorney. He said , "That is the greatest expression of confidence one person can have in another". Then, he explained that I could sign his name on any document that he could sign and it would be just as binding. He was trusting me with his name , his reputation, and everything he owned. I will never betray that confidence. After all, his name is my name.

Mary Ann Martin:

We have tried this all sorts of ways. The first years of our marriage, I took care of the bills. Then, when we started going to church, a preacher said that the husband was to handle the finances. For a while my husband did the books; now it is mine again, but we do it more **together**. Pray about who is going to be the better person at this...work together!

Marriage is such a process of changes. After being together for thirty-seven years and surviving a trip to divorce court, I know anything is possible with our Lord. I have seen Him work mightily.

Vicky Abney:

Have a plan and work together to improve the circumstances or situation. Don't overspend. Pay off your credit card bills 100% every month. Study Dave Ramsey's program, or another financial expert's plan, if you do not handle money well. Growing personal wealth doesn't happen automatically. Only shop when you can afford to buy. A secure financial existence reduces MANY arguments or feelings of uncertainty. Plan for the future, which means you need a college education or technical training that will provide career opportunities. It takes a plan and TONS of money to retire in today's financial market.

Men's Advice on Finances

Louis Ikerd:
Never spend more than you earn. Stay out of debt and only commit to financing your home and cars. Save and pay as you go. Tithe 10% of your earnings and God will provide for all of your needs (not your wants).

Fred Akin:
Finances can kill a marriage at any point. Works out best if one person is in charge. Seems today's couples each have their own accounts. Not making enough and spending too much. Credit cards will usually be the underlying culprit.

Lionel Betancourt:
I do not believe our case would be much different than most, but even with that said, finances can become a factor of strain in every marriage. There will never be enough money to cover everything one wants to do. Spending to get all you want will become a bone of contention. Here is how we dealt with it. Note, I did not say overcame it, but just found a reasonable ground from where to survive.

It was sound advice from my father-in-law, who suggested we keep separate accounts. Each month the money was divided with each one knowing what we were expected to pay for. Understand the division may not have been equal as the mortgage took a bigger bite than some of the other things. We both, for the most of our lives, were wage earners which is what you are as well, right?

The point in this is that neither of us wrote a check with the others knowledge. There simply was no need to tell. On the surface that sounds "sneaky", but we knew where the money was going based on trust. After 48 years, we still have this as our way of "doing business". There is never an argument over money.

Probably all of us realize that there is never enough revenue to take care of all we would like to have. Better cars, houses, fancier places to eat, and such all become part of wanting more. I dare say that even those who make ten times as much as we still run short on occasion simply because we all seem to spend as much or more than we earn. That's life, no matter how foolish it may be.

One last thought – always be aware of the cost of living. For some reason there is a correlation between how much your income rises and the expenses you incur. Expenses will always increase at a faster rate than normal raises in salary. Simply put, when you are given a mandated increase in your wage, say like 10%, the cost of the goods you buy will have to rise by about 12-15%. The manufacturer, distributor, and the retailer cannot, does not, nor will not cover the increase without raising their prices. That is just how the market place functions. It is because of this, an across the board raise will be never be of value. This does not have anything to do with the money you earn for performance in your jobs. That speaks for itself.

E. Don Myers:
We prayed for guidance in all major decisions concerning money. We pay credit cards off each month (in interest or fees). Working with a budget, we gave 10% to our church and later another 10% to building funds (or more), to Texas Baptist Men, Salvation Army, Cancer Fund, etc.

Plan ahead for taxes and insurance and put a little in savings.

Laurel Haas:
This is something that must be done together. You need to pray about finances and follow Gods leading. Be truthful and honest in all your dealings. That is the way you want to be treated by others.

Dempsie Clinton:
It can be a big problem. If you use credit cards, pay them off each month and live on a cash basis. Don't try and keep up with the Jones, just keep up with your income.

Terry D. Hankin:
As we start to share our lives together, so should we share all the monies involved. There is no such thing as *my* money or *your* money but "our" money. Don't forget that paying those bills are to be shared, while giving thanks to the Lord God always.

Mike Sullivan:
I frankly believe that the husband should control the finances unless he is poor at math. That is not to say that the wife cannot participate. The marriage is equal – what belongs to one belongs to both. There is no "I made this money, so it's mine." Especially in the early years, there should be a formal budget. Money can cause more divisions than almost anything. Need to be very careful in handling it.

Ade Fryling:
Financial difficulties is one of the greatest issues that causes disagreement in the marriage. Many divorces are caused by poor financial management and overspending. Credit card debt enslaves many families. Credit card spending can be an important tool for a family. The monthly statement lists all spending, and allows you to be aware of where the money was spent. A smart way to use credit cards is to allocate an amount for total monthly spending. Keep all receipts and add them up weekly to keep your spending on course. Agree together about buying all major items. Be sure money is available, or that monthly payments will fit your budget. Pay off monthly credit card costs. If you can't pay off the card, don't spend excessively until you catch up.

Choose credit cards with the lowest interest rates, and don't be afraid to change cards occasionally to keep the best rate. Save and have at least two months living expenses in a savings account. Anticipate expenses, oil changes, new tires, appliance repairs. Budget envelopes help plan money use and allows for easy payment of rent, groceries and utilities. Couples need to know their expenses and how to pay properly. Share the finances of the home.

All money earned is "our"money. My money or your money should be avoided. Each person is responsible for money spent. Purchases for personal items or personal grooming, haircuts or hair styling should be budgeted. Review together your weekly and monthly spending. Sound quaint? We've been married 54 years, and we have the highest credit rating possible. Take care of your credit. It's OK to buy on time, but never be late in your payments. Never miss a payment! Be diligent in your paying obligations. Select wisely those who supply you with credit.

IN-LAWS

In-Laws

The Last Part of the Package

Chapter 4

This part of getting married is not dealt with in much detail before marriage, but it really should be. Your in-laws, or Mom and Dad as you have been asked to call them, are not anything like your Mom and Dad, for the most part. Most couples are coming from very different backgrounds and now it is time to make all this come together in harmony.

It is always a good sign that your husband is very loving to his mom, which shows you that he has a healthy respect for her and most likely will transfer that respect to you as his wife and mother of his children. The same holds true for a daughter that loves her Dad and that he is her hero. That just means you have met some tough guidelines to be chosen as her husband and the father to her children. That is the ideal, but as you have learned over time, most are not in that category. There are some very dysfunctional families out there in America and your little sweetie may have come from that group. Now, you have to figure out how to learn to love them as your "parents". If you have not been much of a prayer warrior, that may be a-fixin to change!!

You may ask, how am I suppose to love them when they don't love me. They never liked me from the start and years later, it is still the same. Every holiday or get-together is an ordeal. My food was not cooked right or the house is not up to par from their standpoint. Unless you are living under their roof, which I hope that you **aren't,** that will be a temporary situation for the day or weekend. There is a verse that goes… "I can do all things through Christ that strengthens me" Philippians 4:19. Short verse, but it is a powerful one. You can begin the process of giving over your will to God to show forth the love of God when it may not be being returned. These parents raised the person that you love, for better or worse. But, your mate is still the person today that has become who they are 'because of' or in 'spite of' their parents.

God says it is important to *honor* your parents for a long and good life. Some of the quirks about the parents are probably because of their parents….the sins of the Father are passed on to the next generation. If there are some ungodly traits that you cannot be around, then choose your time to be in small increments but lovingly. They are damaged people from things in their past you may not be aware of. Pray that God will give you compassion, wisdom and discernment. Remember, you may be the only person that is praying for that difficult parent/in-law and that Jesus died for them the same as you.

There may be a lot of jealousy and resentment that you came in to the family without their blessing. They just don't get why their child would make any decision without their approval. I like the idea of a guy that will ask the Dad's permission for his daughters hand in marriage. First of all, it shows respect and honor to the parents for a job well done and that they will be included as the on-going part of the new family….not excluded! I can't imagine being excluded from my adult children's new families and from being a grandparent. It is one of the most precious gifts that God gives us in our later years when the nest is empty.

My husband is much better at withholding his advice in their lives than I am. It is like knowing there is going to be a train wreck and you say nothing to prevent it. We have been down that road and don't want the same heartaches to be experienced that we had to go through. I do think it is important to let both sets of parents know that you love them and their advice will be considered, but that the two of you will have to decide what is best for your family.

That really is the premise of this book…advice that you can learn from and avoid our pitfalls. Don't let pride get in your way that you don't need Godly advice. God says that the older women are to help the younger women and older men are to help the younger men. He knew we can't see the road ahead like those that have been down it . So, if you think that parents or in-laws are meddling or trying to control your lives, it may really be that they love you both very much and want the best for you ….they see the train wreck coming! Pray about their advice and ask God to show you what needs to be applied and what needs to be put on the shelf for another day.

What a blessing when the in-laws embrace you as their own and make you feel special. That they are thrilled with the choice that their child made in marrying you. If you are in that kind of family, you are a blessed person and it will bring a balance to your family for all seasons of life. I always liked it when Fred's mom or dad would take my side in an argument. I knew they were feeling protective of me as though I was their own. And I would also see my mom take Fred's side to show him how much she loved him. We miss them now that they are gone, but have some wonderful memories of them being in our lives and our children's lives.

You married your mate because you saw a life of hope and a future… the total package to you. Now, you also have the extended family and that is what makes up the ***Last Part of the Package***.

Women's Advice on In-Laws

Patti Reese:
You have heard the saying that to see what kind of husband a man will be is to look at how he treats his mom. In my case, it is very true. I saw how much he loved, respected and honored his mother. Just because I became his wife did not stop or interfere with him being her son. . We never competed over things (she really is a better cook!) than me.

Jodie Stryker:
Remember, if it were not for your in-laws, you would not have your spouse. Don't think you are competing with each other, but instead remember that you both love the same person.

Vicki Clinton:
You're married now, so you both need to grow-up. Don't pout when you don't get your way and go running back home. You don't need to tell your parents everything about your spouse. Would you want your spouse telling his parents everything? Realize you both are from different backgrounds and you might need to find some common ground. Maybe she's never celebrated Christmas the way your family always celebrates. Even the joys of Christmas can become a heated debate with sometimes juggling 2, 3 or 4 sets of in-laws.

Sandra Dean:

Ladies, never say anything bad about your husband to your mother. You will forget about it later because you love him. She won't and it can ruin your marriage. Trust me. That was a big problem in my first marriage. I learned better in my second marriage. When my mother said something derogatory about my husband , I immediately stood up to her and told her never to put him down in my presence again. She never did and it made a big difference in my second marriage.

Anonymous:

It's his mother/father/sister/brother. Be nice to them. Support your spouse. If it is your mother/father/sister/brother, remember your spouse comes first.

Pat Fryling:

When we married we moved away from home due to jobs. After all, going to college and training for a career was important and you had to go where it was best for you. I never really had a problem with my in-laws, which I am very thankful for. We are not your parents, but your husband's parents. Treat us with kindness and respect as you would with your own parents and that love goes a long way.

Debbie Morris:

This was one of the biggest challenges in our marriage. My mother-in-law was a very difficult woman to deal with. I never confronted her, because I was afraid she would make it hard on me and my husband.

Sylvia Hankin:

You won't always agree with them, accept their advice, and thank them. Pray for your spouses parents, spend time with them, and always make them feel welcomed in your home.

Kay Carol Pemberton:
Being accepted by your husband's mother can be very difficult. After all, a young wife is replacing his mother in many ways. Time tends to show a difficult mother-in-law that the wife is loving and caring. Respect in-laws even when you don't feel they respect you.

Barbara Sullivan:
Prepare to learn from your mother-in-law. She knows and loves your husband.

Plan to NEVER accuse your husband to your mother-in-law. You may want to, but always recall she is his loving Mom (just as you'd want your Mom to be your advocate or defender).

Actually his family may lend great stability to your home as they "expect" much of him (and have his whole life – he really does not want to disappoint them as you don't want to disappoint your family).

They will do things different than your parents. In these areas, God is pushing for balance that is not too extreme or too complacent.

Vicky Abney:
Girls can be pretty close to their families. Guys tend to leave and cleave. I worked hard to be careful about time spent with my sisters and mother. Paul seemed to appreciate this. He thought they were very supportive and loving, but he liked the balance of "us"…us and extended family… us and friends. Thank your in-laws (be sincere) when they are supportive of you. Invite them over, show kindness. Make special traditions with them.

Frances Knight:
I was blessed to have wonderful in-laws. As a bride, one of the first things that Normah Knight said to me was, "Don't ever introduce me as your mother-in-law and I will never refer to you as my daughter-in-law." She became my "Mom" and I became a second daughter. This was almost providential since my sweet mother was killed in a car wreck shortly thereafter. For the next fifty-four years, my new "Mom" was my only mother.

Men's Advice on In-Laws

Louis Martin:
Almost everyone has them. You got to take the good with the bad. You both knew what you were getting into, I would think. I was blessed with great in-laws. Times got rough because of health problems. But the love for these folks over the years and the love both my wife and I had for each other endured. Together we were able to take care of the mother and father until their death. God had a lot to do with this with answered prayer. Thanks. On the other side, my parents lived so far away we had few problems. WITH THE LORD IN YOUR LIFE YOU CAN ALWAYS BE HAPPY!!!

Larry Pemberton:
Communicating your love and desire for happiness with their daughter is very important. Showing that you are a Godly man and respect their daughter will go a long way to gain respect from the in-laws.

Dempsie Clinton:
Your in-laws are your spouse's family, so that makes them your family. Treat them as your family and not as "in-laws."

Terry D. Hankin:
In-laws are going to be a part of your lives, so make the best of it. They can make it easy or tense in your relationship with your spouse. Don't allow them to rule your lives, but allow them to be a part of it whenever possible. Remember that they are a part of your spouse as well as children.

Ade Fryling

I have to realize that relations with in-laws can be the greatest challenge in the marriage relationship. My mother-in-law was a gifted, clever, strong willed and a "make happen" person. My personality is similar, so we were destined for confrontation. When Pat and I married, we moved five hours from her family and from mine as well. We had the privilege to learn to live in love without family influence.

I soon learned to love Pat's Mom and Dad because they respected us and our marriage. As a Mother or Father-in-law, it is important to give our children space when they marry. Work at training your children to choose mates that share the same values, same spiritual position, and certainly a financially mature person. You will have an easier time with the in-laws if indeed your life position and purpose is close to theirs. On that basis there will be less reason for conflict.

We have resolved to be available when needed and try to be of help when we are together. Each in-law situation is certainly different and although I am trained in Psychology, the training has only given us a foundation on building a friendly relationship. In dealing with in-laws, be an understanding, outgoing individual and be happy with any positive outflow from them. Be patient for the in-laws to accept you, do it for your mate by loving them.

Louis Ikerd:

When you marry, in-laws are part of the package. Let them be a part of your family, but they should know that your spouse is number one.

Mike Sullivan:

Obviously we are to love our extended family. However, when married we do leave mom and dad and cling to one another. When troubles arise, do not run to mom or dad for comfort or even for guidance. Your guide is the Holy Spirit. Sharing troubles with relatives or anyone else can only expand the problems. Think before speaking. Be sure that nothing derogatory is said about your mate to parents. Visit when possible, trying not to show favoritism.

Fred Akin:

My wife comes from a large family of six and they have become my family, too. I had a Mother-in-law, Grandma, that never interfered in our business. She had a lot of reason to add in her opinion, but she never did. Having in-laws has been a great experience, as we all get together every year and have a great time.

RAISING CHILDREN

Raising Children

"What Have We Gotten Ourselves Into?"

Chapter 5

There is a natural progression for most marriages to eventually want to have children. Some couples have children right away, and for others it may be years down the road. Whatever the time frame is in your journey, mark it down, it will never be the same as before! You have made a permanent decision to start sharing your lives with another, called a child. You are now going to look at life through another set of eyes that will teach you to be in awe of the smallest things that you had not really stopped to even think about before. There will be a compassion come from you that you had not shown to others, a tenderness for this 'little soul' that is a combination of you and your spouse. Entertainment will take on a whole new meaning as this child is the most amusing, delightful and smartest child in the world. This information is always verified by all sets of doting grandparents.

You read all the books necessary about raising children (ours was Dr. Spock), so now you are ready for every challenge. Well, almost every challenge. The primary caretaker will normally be the mom as she tends to the baby for months. I am delighted to see the Dads taking on responsibilities with the newborn, but there does seem to be an innate fear when the baby is under 6 months to actually take on the baby for a whole day to give mom a break. There is a video out on America's Funniest Home Videos about Dad's changing a diaper that is unbelievable. Dads are throwing up, wearing gas mask, fainting, gagging , wearing a space suit…... if you can Google this video, it will make your day. Fred would not even attempt to change a diaper, as he would gag and want to throw up. It was amazing that he never heard the baby cry at 2:00am to help with a night feeding….that is called selective hearing!

That was fairly normal in the 60's and 70's. Today the Dads are more hands on from seeing the birth, cutting the cord and getting up for night feedings…still resistance with the dirty diaper. It's not that moms like changing them either, but it is written in the MOM Handbook that it is your sworn duty, otherwise we would get out of the job, too!!! Dads are also taking off work for several weeks to help Mom and baby get settled in at home.

If you have an opportunity to see your child being born, then pursue it with the doctors. It is so impacting, this miracle of miracles that God provides for us. It is a precious experience that makes moms and dads acknowledge who God is and that He is in charge of life. The world takes on new meaning of God being Omnipotent , Omnipresence and Sovereign. At that moment your child is born, you realize that He cares for humanity and is compassionate. Don't minimize or forget that prayer is a vital part of birth, as the process has many twists and turns that can happen. That is just the beginning of the long journey of raising a child.

You are going to see a prayer life with new dimensions as you *worry* over every cold, bump and bruise. Every hurdle that your child comes against in life also becomes your hurdle as you want to protect them from failure and disappointment. It is your privilege to pray with them and for them. Life's lessons will teach them how to draw strength from God, as they will come across difficult situations as long as they live in this world, just as we do.

Parents begin to realize that there is a child watching their every move to see how they react with life's struggles. They will imitate this since you are their role model. Our language gets a strong 'Lysol' clean-up due to little ears listening and repeating all we say and how we say it. It doesn't take long for a kindergarten teacher to get a view of their students home life as she listens to them talk and watches them react to other children. Each child is usually a vivid picture of what kind of job we are doing at home in all areas.

There are no perfect parents! You aren't one and neither were your parents. In fact there is no perfect person, other than Jesus Christ. Having that information will now allow you to stop beating yourself up when you have really blown it. I wish I could tell you that wasn't going to happen, but it will happen many, many times. There will be times that you need to ask your children to forgive you. This is a powerful lesson in learning to admit your mistakes and that if it has hurt someone that you need to ask forgiveness. It is also a picture of how God will always forgive us no matter how many times we have failed Him.

Parents need to be united in raising their children. That means you will need to pray together about all that is happening to them and seeking God's Word to direct your path for the right answers. Parents have come from different backgrounds of what is the right and wrong way to raise a child. That is why it will take prayer to bring you together to agree on what is the best solution for each situation. Talk to other Godly parents and grandparents about how they have handled certain situations and learn from them. This is where your parents and church becomes a vital source for direction. It really is true of the saying that "it takes a village to raise a child". You are not in this world alone to try and get this parenting challenge figured out. God intended you to let the extended families you came from and your church family be a support to your efforts. I am so glad that we had both to help us as we raised our children. I know they turned out so well because of those extended families in our lives....we couldn't have done it without them.

As time progresses through each stage of your children's lives, you will reach that point where it is time to *let them go*. You have taught them spiritually and mentally what they needed to survive in a world of unknowns and they are now officially adults. I didn't say your job as a parent is over....it is never over! You will always w*orry* over their next step and still want to protect them like they are still your little child. But a good parent soon learns that they are out of the nest and God becomes their over-seeing parent.

You almost pray more now than before, because they are out of your home and on their own. Before, you had a watchful eye on them and now you have to *trust* that God will be watching out for them on their new adventure of being an adult. It is a proud moment when you get to see them as they graduate from high school and college, take that first real job, buy their own car, pick their mate, get married and now have their own children. Life has come full circle and hopefully you will get to be a part of this next phase in their journey. You will then be glad to say : Yes, I do know ***"What we have gotten ourselves into!"***

Women's Advice on Raising Children

Elma Naranjo:
I believe it is so important to raise children in God's principals. A child should be loved unconditionally and learn what love is by example. Tell your child daily he is loved. "I love you" and "I am so proud of you" are statements your child should hear every single day. When they fail, disappoint, or just mess up, first remember that we are imperfect beings and that we have done our own messing up. Second, discipline and talk about it. Yes, he is a child, but he is a person too, a person that deserves that time with you. Never let your child have an instant of doubt of your love and support in spite of circumstances that may arise.

Mary Ann Martin:
Coming from a home of a lot of bickering, I have always made it my goal not to argue in front of our children. There are times when you grit your teeth, but we have always tried to discuss later whatever we disagreed on.

Sandra Dean:
Study your child's personality type and learn their strengths and weakness as well as their emotional needs. This is crucial information that you must have to encourage, equip, train, and discipline your children. Just because you are a certain way does not mean they are or should be. Proverbs 22:6

Jodie Stryker:
Be quick to make right and apologize. Teach your children that we can be wrong and that is okay; teach them how to say "I'm sorry." Model this behavior so it is second nature to them.

Anonymous:
One person has to be the bad guy, **take turns**. Your kids don't need another friend; they need parents who set clear parameters; always live up to your word; and love them unconditionally and forever. Take time to play with them. The house and chores will always be there; they won't. Early and often, get on your knees and give your children to God. God will guide your actions and words if you will let Him.

Vicki Clinton:
Love, love, love. The most important thing you can do for your child is love and respect your spouse. With the foundation strong, the children will sense the stability and love. Don't underestimate the children's ability to discern, even very young. I think it is of the utmost importance that parents be in complete agreement on disciplining the child, especially in front of the child. Have a private conversation with spouse, prior to disciplining

Patti Reese:
- Pray much. Pray often. Each child is so unique and it is a learning process the entire time you are raising them. Even with their best interest at heart, we don't always get it right. I have told my kids on more than one occasion that Adam and Eve had a perfect "parent" and they still messed up!
- Love them with all your heart and tell them everyday. They may not always act like they believe you or even act like they care, but tell them anyway.
- Discipline them. Be sure they are allowed to suffer the consequences of the choice they make. Don't always "save" them. Sometimes we are more afraid of the consequences than they are.

- Understand the difference between an accident (don't shame a child or lose your cool over a glass of spilled milk) and deliberate disobedience or rebellion.
- Give them freedom to fail and to learn from those experiences. Having our own children gives us such an insight to our relationship with our Heavenly Father.
- Nurture their spiritual needs. "Train up a child in the way he should go (the way God designed him) and when he is old he will not depart from it." Pray with them. It's another way for them to see your relationship with your Father and to talk to them about their spiritual life.
- Read to them for as long as they will let you. Another great avenue of communication with your kids.

Debbie Morris:
After a busy day of work or school, dinner around the table is the most important time of the day. A download from everyone gives time to reflect and understand what each person may be going through, both good and bad. And be sure and listen!

Kay Carol Pemberton:
Two words come to mind: prayer and patience. Raising children is not an easy task. Without God's help it is impossible. Patience is most important in dealing with children and especially teenagers. Parents must not give up no matter how difficult the challenge.

Mary Anne Betancourt:
I want to share about child rearing: That is the hardest thing about marriage or about life, including owning and managing three retail shops. I wish I could do it over. What I would do is:
- Spend more time asking the Lord's advice;
- Spend more time playing with them;
- Being sure everyday I tell them God loves them. They are worth much in His eyes and in mine.

Netta White:
It is a great disservice to your children if you do not discipline them. When they don't know the boundaries of right and wrong, acceptable and unacceptable behavior, their actions will not only reflect on you, the parent, but affect your children's relations with other people. e.g. We invited a couple over with their 3 children for dinner one evening. The children ate their dinner quickly and wanted to watch TV. We were still eating dinner, but instead of watching TV, they were jumping up and down on our sofas. The parents never said a word to them to stop. I could hardly concentrate on dinner, so I went over and told them to sit down because I was afraid they might fall and hurt themselves. Well, they discovered our little dog's toys, so they started throwing the toys across the room at each other. (The youngest one, about 18 months, wasn't so bad) I was afraid they were going to break something. Finally, the father told them not to do that. It was very difficult to enjoy the parents who were such nice people. The kids ran into the other rooms in our house – bedrooms and computer room – back and forth. I was a nervous wreck! I was trying to rush dinner so we could go outside and sit on the porch. The children ran in and out of our house, leaving the doors open or slamming them. It was such a relief when they left! Needless to say, I would never invite them over again, and if I did, it would be adults only.

Would you like to invite this family over to your house for dinner? The sad thing is, it's not the children's fault. They were not taught how to behave properly. Love your children enough to discipline them, this way, other people will enjoy and love them too!

Discipline your children, whether you spank them or use time out. Children need boundaries to grow up feeling safe and secure.

A dear friend used to tell me, you have to hold your children accountable – if you say you're going to do something – follow through with it – have them face the consequences of their actions! Teach your children manners – how they act is a reflection on you.

Pat Fryling:
Being a parent is one of the most rewarding responsibilities you can have in life. Before you decide to have children, make sure you are ready for this lifetime commitment and have the time it takes to raise these gifts you are given. To me it is the most wonderful treasure and gift you can receive in life. A child needs you full time, it really falls on the mother

as she is the nurturing parent and the child usually runs to her. Be ready with open arms to care, correct, and love even when you are tired , sick , feeling stressed , having a bad day, or just wanting some time to yourself. It's wonderful when you have a husband that truly understands your need for a shopping trip alone or a girls night out. We usually feel guilty when we ask for time for ourselves, but you need to take care of yourself. There will be time later in life when you have an empty nest and wish you could go back. Enjoy the moments you have with your children, listen to them, love them and respect them and you will receive all these wonderful things in return. Children are a gift from God, treat them as so.

Sylvia Hankin:
Children are blessings from the LORD, so please bring them up the way God would want you to. Mom, Dad, remember that you're a parent first and then a friend. Teach them to behave first at home as well as in public. Yes, they are kids, but they need to learn manners from early childhood. Pray for them daily. Share the Word of God with them.

Vicky Abney:
Have a plan and work hard at making every day important. Loving your kids means teaching, leading, mentoring, explaining, modeling, assuring, providing for, and helping on an endless array of topics. Build a very close bond with your child, but stay in the parent role until your kids are grown, then transition to the "friend" stage. Be bold in teaching your kids about money management, budgeting, doing chores and regular maintenance. (You don't want to raise lazy kids).

When your kids are adults, love them by giving them space. Children are blessings and very special fruits of a great marriage.

P.S. Paul always let me know subtly, I came first, before the kids.

Barbara Sullivan:
Love them, appreciate them, tell them they are a gift from God. Lead, guide, direct and correct from the position of unconditional love , which is how Christ does it. Be a parent – let friends be friends. Don't live through your children. It is too much responsibility and pressure for them "to succeed" to fulfill our unrequited dreams.

Money spent on children NEVER replaces time spent with them (even when teens seem to prefer peers – stand your ground and keep family doing the things together.) Go faithfully to support them in their activities, even the ones where they don't shine. This is a good time to share when you didn't "shine" either. Point out talents, abilities, accomplishments. For every criticism try to balance it with compliments on strengths.

Let them know that God put them in this family. They are like a piece of coal becoming a diamond and that is why there is parental pressure. Let them earn money for "stuff" they want, but really don't need…. like expensive trendy clothes and techy items. I was reared with an allowance for chores philosophy which flows into work for pay. I am against child modeling. Too much pressure and eventually too much power (as they bring in money). A cute 5 year old will have growth spurts, big teeth, a thickening body and pimples. Thus the princess can become rejected by these same people and easy money is gone.

If you were reared by a screamer/yeller, ask God to deliver you from using this same tactic.

Fight for your family devotionals each day. It will be a fight almost everyday as Satan does not want that foundation to be built. Persevere for your children and the family. Be sure to be "transparent" and honest about needs, fears, problems and blessings. They will face all of this later – give them coping skills. Teach them to pray to God for all their needs.

I recommend sports – more eyes and more accountability helps keep them on the right track. Also it builds team work (such as marriage), self confidence and stretches their abilities in a safe environment (even if they get hurt – maybe they'll become a Physical Therapist)

Reveal by actions, time, efforts, supports, money and prayers of the importance of Christ and His Church. Actions speak louder than words!

Do not overlook excuses or condone lying or stealing – it grows life fungus.

Encourage outside interests like dance, karate, piano, church youth activities, and little jobs. Especially, if school activities like sports, band or drama don't "fit" your child.

Men's Advice on Raising Children

Mike Sullivan:
First, there must be consistency. Mom cannot override Dad, or vice versa. Parental examples weigh much heavier than parental words. Normally, mothers do most of the raising. The father must have an active part from the beginning and continue through life. In the case of more than one child... again equality. Each treated the same. Scriptures tell us to " Raise up a child in the way of the Lord and when they grow old, they will not depart from it."

Laurel Haas:
Children are a true gift from God and we need to raise them according to God's plan. We raised them the best we knew how with true love. When they are older we gave them our blessings to go to college, get jobs, married and trust them to God more.

Again, God is first in raising our children. They must be raised in Church.

Duane Stryker:
If you disagree with how your spouse is handling a situation, tell her in private. It is important to have a united front and for your children to know that you are both on the same page.

Louis Ikerd:
This is a joint venture. Children need to see consistency from both parents concerning love, discipline and structure in the home. Commit your children to God for they are His. Seek His wisdom in all areas of raising your children. Attend church regularly with your children, as this example lets them know how important it is to have a relationship with God and His Son.

Fred Akin:
I always told my kids that I loved them and that I was proud of them. I made sure that I supported them in any activity that they were involved in. That was also what my parents did for me as I was growing up.

I think that kids today are spending too much time in front of computers and messing with gadgets...they need to get outside and learn to play.

Some of our best family memories were spent going to the beach and playing all day....no phones, no computers, but just learning to enjoy each other and spending quality time together.

Harry Reese:
Children are a precious gift from God and should be treated as such with much prayer. They should know they have the freedom to fail and still be cherished. The biblical command is for parents to train their child and for the child to learn obedience. Required reading is James Dobsons' book: Dare to Discipline.

Ade Fryling:
Beside the couple's relationship, children and the training of them is the couple's greatest responsibility. Having children is both a joy and a challenge to the relationship. Holding each child for the first time and sharing that joy together is one of the deepest blessings of the union. Realizing that this child is the result of a deep intimate union, and also is one of the purposes that God gave us sexual relations Children that are produced by that intimate relationship with love at its' core, will be nourished both physically and emotionally to be complete individuals, confident and independent.

- The smallest child needs love, shown by holding, feeding, bathing, talking to, so that the child will bond with the difference voices. Children enjoy water and bathing can be an enjoyable time for both of you.
- Children need structure and discipline. Discipline is discussed, decided and implemented through agreement by both parents. There can be no disagreement between the parents when discipline is given.
- Discipline must be given to change the habit of the child, never to personally injure the child.
- Discipline always ends in loving the child by telling them that you love them, but dislike the attitude or habit they display.
- Praising the good habits is an important encouragement toward change, and lifts the spirit of the child toward good.
- Disobedience is always an offense against the parent, and ultimately toward God.
- The most important training of a child is to introduce them to God as the highest authority. God will love them unconditionally and forgive any offense if they ask Him and are truly sorry for the offense.
- All children must be trained over time to be confident in their decisions through a mature thinking process, based on personal belief and practice based on Bible principles.
- The goal of the parents is to produce a loving and compassionate adult who is independent and confident in meeting the challenges of life.

Louis Martin:

Today is not like it used to be! I am still a firm believer in spare the rod, spoil the child. Most parents today do not. They have things like time out. Teach them right from wrong. When they are wrong, they need to get a spanking and be sure to tell them why. When they are right, praise them on how good they are. Children should know that their parents love them and know that their parents love each other. Give them lots of Hugs and Kisses.

J.B. Morris:
Be selective with what you get your kids involved in. Don't feel they need to compete or be involved in everything! Let them choose one or two things they really enjoy, and don't let it be activities that interfere with church activities as a family.

Dempsie Clinton:
You need to understand your child's temperament. Children will react to your voice. If you always tell them no three times before you get serious, they know that. Go to the child, have them look at you, face to face, and tell them what you want them to do. Be positive in what you say. If you reinforce the negative, that is what they will remember. The coach doesn't tell his football players "don't drop the ball", he tells them "to catch the ball."

Larry Pemberton:
Keep your eyes wide open! When you see potential problems with children/teens, seek professional help immediately. Know what your kids are doing at all times. Know their friends. Be visible and show them you are interested and watching them. Don't be a friend, be a parent!

James Dean:
Set boundaries and tell them what you expect. Parenting is not about being your kid's friend, you are in authority over them, act like it. Punish bad behavior and reward good behavior. It is never fun to be the bad guy, but your heartaches will be mild compared to the pain that will come later if your child does not understand rules and the consequences.

Raising kids is not about making them happy. It is preparing them to be responsible adults. Rewards without hard work and effort enforce an entitlement mentality. Do not always rescue them, they need to experience failure as well as success.

Spend time with them. Dropping them off at ball practice or dance lessons is not spending time with them. If you cannot coach or teach, stay and watch. The more time you spend with them, the better off they are going to be during adolescence.

Find hobbies or activities they like, not what you did not get to do growing up. Understand their strengths and weakness and help develop a positive attitude about trying new things. If you are lucky enough to find hobbies you both like, then it will be easier to teach and model the proper behavior about how to handle successes, fairness, humility and confidence.

Kids learn from what you do, not what you say. If you start a project, then finish it. Don't just do the fun stuff and quit. Life is not fair. Let them see you push through the tough times to complete a task.

Ron White:

Spend quality time with your children – you are creating precious memories for them. Let them know you love and care for them. When your child makes a commitment, make sure they follow through with it.

Teach them that their word is their bond. It is the one thing no one can take away from them.

Terry D. Hankin:

First, there is no such thing as a perfect child. Second, remember that children are constantly learning and testing their own limits as well as yours. Third, remember, you should be in control. There is no instruction manual on perfect parenting, so do the best you can do with God in your lives.

SURVIVING A CRISIS

Surviving A Crisis

Built on sand or the Rock?

Chapter 6

There will be times in every marriage that a crisis will happen. The dictionary says that a 'crisis' is : a dangerous or worrying time; a critical moment; a disaster; catastrophe; emergency; calamity; predicament! It can come at you from many directions; some that are brought on from yourselves and others that will just be part of living in this world.

There will be your parents and grandparents death, which will be one of the hard times that all will face. It could be the sickness or death of a child. This will probably be one of the most emotional of all tests or crisis you will ever deal with. It could be losing your home to fire or storms, or losing your home because of job loss. I have seen many couples go through a serious illness, such as cancer or heart attack or some mysterious illness that there is no name for. Car wrecks happen every day that cause bodily injury or sometimes death. There can be infidelity, drinking or gambling by one of the partners that will leave its scars on all that know them. Your kids may get involved with the wrong group that are doing drugs. There will be heartache as a parent watches their child go to prison for a stupid, senseless mistake that cannot be undone. You may be the by-product of a company that is downsizing and you have been given your termination letter. Some couples face the downward spiral of their mate fighting depression; there seems to be no hope that they will ever see them normal again. There is

HOPE in any of these situations, but it will take time and healing of the soul. You can survive this! You will survive this! But the question is....... what will you learn from surviving this crisis?

When you took your wedding vows, you said "for better or worse, in sickness and in health". Those words were put there because you will face situations that are going to test who you really are as a person and what your marriage is made of. You say those vows and hope that you will be that couple that is never going to go down those sad roads that life can bring into your wonderful, perfect home, because you love each other so much. I would love to tell you that is true, but I am here to bring life into a reality check. There will be great and wonderful events, but also hard and sad events. Sometimes they are happening at the same time!

There is a great song that goes: "One day at a time, sweet Jesus, that's all I'm asking from You". We have no promises that life will be a bed of roses because we are Christians. It does mean that God will take everything that happens in your life and will hold your hand and give you strength to get through the hard times. A verse in Romans 8:28 says that "ALL things work together for good to them that are called according to His purpose". First of all, this is a promise to a Christian that God knows what you are facing and wants you to bring it to Him, so that you can begin the process of learning what *good* He is going to bring out of this trial. He will give you strength and courage that is supernatural because He is a supernatural Person that created you. This is when your prayer life will go into a deep growth, because you **don't** have the answers how to get this crisis turned around , except by the grace of God. You will begin to search out scriptures in His Word that you didn't know existed, because you have got to have some answers from on High. He will teach you patience to wait on Him, and not to run ahead of Him. You will learn about the Sovereignty of God, as you realize, that in some cases, this is not going to end as you have been praying for it to. Crisis will either push you toward God or very far away in your anger at Him. It is okay to be angry with God as you begin to process this answer is not the one you wanted.... WHY God is this happening to me or to my family?? It's okay to be angry, but also important to not stay there in your anger. This is where you must ask what am I going to learn from this?

When sin entered into the picture from Adam and Eve, that is when the perfect picture was taken away. Sin will now be a part of this world that you and I are living in until we pass from this life. This trial may be caused by your own doing or it came into your life through someone or something else. Regardless, it has affected your life and you are very angry about it. Anger does terrible things to a person's personality and to their health. We were not created to carry or bury that anger in our lives….it will have consequences! They say that a high percentage of people in the hospitals and mental institutions are there because of unresolved issues in their lives. Some are situations from early childhood. There are pastors, counselors and psychiatrist that are trained to help you get through these hard times. Please be careful about medications as these are used to dull us from the pain, which at some point will have to be dealt with and processed through. It will take time and we must give God that time to begin to heal our hearts from the pain.

I can tell you that all these couples that have shared their lives in this book have gone through some tough times, and God will use people like them in your lives at your own church to pray with you, cry with you and be there for you to talk with. Another great verse is in 2 Corinthians 1:3-4. Basically, it is saying that if you have gone through a hard trial , that God will bring His comfort to you and then it is our "calling" to help someone else that is going through that same problem. You see, it becomes a ministry in your life because you actually do understand what that person is going through like no one else can know. They need to know that you are a survivor of that crisis, by the grace of God, and that somehow life will have a light at the end of this dark tunnel with time. Time…a four letter word that is small, but it gives HOPE to us if we will just hang in there and watch God begin to bring some good out of this trial as He promised He would.

This is where your faith kicks in, that you have trusted your life to a God that loves you and knows of your pain. Pain that will be there because of sin coming into this world. Remember that Satan has come to "steal, kill and destroy" and God allows him in this world so we can choose right from wrong and good over bad. He gave us a free will to choose if we want to know His love through the death of His Son Jesus on the cross. That He paid the price for those sins, so that we can be brought to God blameless through the shed blood of Christ. A perfect Christ that went to the cross for a sinful world. That is why He is called the Lamb of God. He was the sacrifice that we could never be, because we are not perfect. Now you see the bigger picture of where this is all going. One day you will go to heaven, if you have chosen Him, where there will be no more pain or crying or death. That is His promise to us as His children. Read John 14:1-6 about Heaven.

We are created beings that are in this world for a purpose that God has designed for our lives. We can choose to wade through this crazy world and make decisions that we think are the best. Remember that God is Omniscient and He alone knows what is down that path ahead of us and can guide us in the right direction. I can't imagine where my life would be if I had not prayed and asked God to show me through His Word and seeking Christian advice what to do. Why would I ever want to jump into the unknown waters without Him going before me…He is throwing me a lifeline, if I will choose to trust Him! I have prayed and asked God to open or shut doors for many decisions, as I never want to be without His covering of blessing in my life. His directions will always be for the best in my life as no one loved me more… Period!! I pray and also ask God to show me through the protective covering of my husband, that He will speak wisdom through him to guide our family.

To sum up this chapter, I want to encourage you that God is watching over you in the good and the bad. No one wants to go through hard times! No one wants to be brought out of that comfort zone of security that we build for our lives. This is where we must decide if our lives are *"Built on sand or the Rock"?*

Women's Advice on Surviving a Crisis

Barbara Sullivan:
My Mom used to say that I'd look back and laugh. I prefer to look back and testify to the goodness of the Lord in the land of the living. God does work to save marriages.

Some of our closest times were when we were in a financial or health mess. Close to each other and close to God (I never forgot to pray and listen during these testing times.) God's solutions were often miracles "just in the nick of time." These are faith building times.

I would often go outside and address the evil one, rebuking him if outside circumstances were threatening (like hurricanes, health, money not being paid). If it was our own stupidity or foolishness, I asked for mercy and help and forgiveness.

Elma Naranjo:
We will all face hard times which is why it is so important to commit our life and our marriage to the Lord. We need to pray daily and seek His guidance as we live our daily lives. Read His word daily, attend church and bible studies so that you can grow in the Christian life. God says in Hosea 4:6 Our people perish for lack of knowledge. In the Word there is promises for every need in our lives. We need to claim these promises so we can live abundant and fulfilled lives.

Mary Ann Martin:
You will have crisis come your way.. Some will seem bigger than others. Prayer and good friends and counseling are some ways to get through. Stick by each other. Again, even during a crisis, take time for each other. Talk, go for walks in the mall, sometimes it's just good to get out of the house to talk.

Jodie Stryker:
The book of Hebrews tells us to encourage one another. In the midst of a crisis, pray and encourage your spouse even more so. Remember, this too shall pass!

Anonymous:
Don't be a drama queen. If it's truly a crisis, pray first. Talk to each other. It is difficult to get a husband to talk about problems. Men are usually problem solvers, and sometimes come across as dictatorial; women usually want to talk it through, hash and rehash, and finally make a decision. Both of you have to give a little and understand how each works through a crisis. It is important to make a decision that this crisis will not drive you apart, but will draw you together and make your relationship stronger.

Sandra Dean:
Pray for wisdom. Make a decision together. Support each other in the decision and do not allow it to be divisive in your marriage. It can draw you closer together. Remember to always be each other's biggest fan. Eccl. 4;12b

Pat Fryling:
This is where your faith is tested. Always remember that God is in control. He knows your every need, desire, concern; bring it to Him in prayer, asking for His direction, His guidance. Do not put the blame on any one or any thing; ask what Jesus would do and suck it up and do it. I know it sounds harsh but God always has a purpose in everything we do. Sometimes things are easy and sometimes hard, but it's the hard things

that can get us out of kilter. That is what Satan is waiting for, we cannot give in to him. We have to be strong and together, no matter how hard it may be.

Patti Reese:
- I do not know how anyone survives a crisis without the Lord. Trusting him and his word, believing Him and His word. Remembering his faithfulness in the smaller things prepares you for trusting Him in a big crisis. It's another reason to be an active part of the local church body, the body is there to help in times of need (the way God designed it). Sometimes you are the giver and sometimes you are the recipient.
- On your knees! In Prayer! In His Word! Waiting expectantly for Him to work, to give you peace through the storm, for Him to deliver you out of the storm in His perfect timing.
- Trusting the Lord "that all things work together for good to them that love the Lord and are called according to His purpose." Romans 8:28.

Frances Knight:
Every long marriage will eventually face deaths in a family. First, my mother was killed in a car wreck when she was 43 and I was 20. When I thought that my world had come to an end, I had my young husband's shoulder to cry on. I will always be grateful to him for helping me through that dark time.

Years later , our first son died at age 38. The pain was so deep I could hardly breathe. It is easy to become so enmeshed in your own grief, that you do not fully realize that Dad is suffering too. Recovery is a long process. Be patient with each other.

A serious word of caution. I was walking down the hospital hall with a chaplain whose granddaughter drowned in their swimming pool. She was worried about their daughter and her husband. She said ," Most of the time when a couple loses a child, they eventually get a divorce. They blame each other in some way."

Kay Carol Pemberton:
Woman tend to be the strength in a lot of crisis situations. I have had to learn not to be frustrated with my husband in difficult times. Sometimes men just don't know what to do or how to help or give comfort. Teach them!

Sylvia Hankin:
This is where you become closer than ever, pray together, cry together and praise together. Be patient and remember that everything that happens, God is aware of. Don't blame one another or anyone else. This doesn't mean you won't have hurt feelings or confusion; that is part of being human.

Vicki Clinton:
When a crisis comes, this is a time for the two of you to grow together and become stronger as a couple. In these times you will learn more about the heart of your spouse. Learn from each and every crisis what your spouse's special needs are. Be there for each other, mentally and physically. You know what you need most; tell your spouse, nobody is a mind reader.

Phyllis Haas:
This is something that must be worked on at all times. Everyone has a crisis at one time or another. Remember to Pray about it is the first thing to do. Then wait and listen to God. PRAYER is essential in ALL things.

We can all think if we had done this or that would have been better. Learn from your mistakes at the time. PRAY about everything…nothing is too small for God.

Debbie Morris:
It will happen! At some point you WILL experience something that causes great stress on your marriage. During that time you must encourage your mate, and rely upon God to get you both through it. Don't point fingers. Don't blame. Just work through it. Time heals a lot of wounds.

Men's Advice on Suriving a Crisis

Ade Fryling:

A marriage relationship is never without problems, some of which will reach crisis proportions. There are many kinds of crisis, but all crisis can eventually seriously test the marriage relationship. All crisis must be addressed together. This is a useful approach.

1. God knows your difficulty, ask for His help. Ask Him to show you the right way.

2. Write out the problem and all the extending issues that go with it.

3. What are good solutions, actions to start with, actions to improve the problem, actions to complete the issue.

4. Who will address the issue, what will be required of both to have success in the end.

5. If it is a personal crisis, the partner needs to be willing to give needed support, whether it be work, arranging details, and support in every area.

6. A good partner is alert to changing needs and adjusts input as needed.

7. Emotional health is a constant importance for both partners. Making sure the responsibility is shared, and that feelings are shared and discussed. Be alert for signs of discouragement, left unattended will lead to depression, isolation and despondency.

8. Crisis happens when indicators of need are ignored.

Harry Reese:
When a crisis occurs; pray first! Rely on scripture: "All things work together for good to those who love the Lord and are called according to His purpose." Rom 8:28.

"Be anxious for nothing, but in everything by prayer and supplication, with thanksgiving, make your requests known to the Lord and the peace of God, which transcends all understanding, will guard your heart and mind in Christ Jesus." Philippians 4:6-7

"Be joyful always, pray continually; give thanks in all circumstances, for this is God's will for you in Christ Jesus. I Thes 5:16

Our joy, praise and thankfulness should not fluctuate with our circumstances or feelings.

Larry Pemberton:
My wife is my strength. She is so strong in difficult situations and I tend to step back. Men need to be compassionate and stay by their spouse's side and offer whatever help is needed in every situation. Prayer is the greatest way to do this.

Dempsie Clinton :
Whatever the crisis, pray, pray, pray. Stay on your knees, God answers knee-mail.

Duane Stryker:
Marriage is not a 50/50 arrangement. When your spouse is in the middle of a crisis, the arrangement may be 95/5. Pray and remember that the valleys are where we grow as individuals and as couples.

Louis Ikerd:
Truly there will be times of crisis for all families. This is when husbands and wives really need to come together as one, seeking God's council through prayer and to let go of self. Families that work through the unpleasant issues of life usually have a stronger marriage.

Mike Sullivan:
All of us go through crisis. If we really have faith that God will meet our needs, that He will never leave us nor forsake us, then we also should know that we should be anxious for nothing, but in everything by prayer, make our request known to God (Philippians4:4-7). If we can concentrate on the fact that He is ultimately in charge, we can rest in Him. Instead of making our circumstances worse, we should wait on His direction, then we'll be successful.

Fred Akin:
God is always in control of all situations. When you are in a crisis, surround yourself with family and close friends. I have always said that "things" happen for a reason. You have to find out what that reason is to find peace about it.

Terry D. Hankin:
We don't like to deal with this, but it is almost always unavoidable. Lean on and comfort each other as you stand together against whatever comes with God always on your side. God allows it to test our faith in Him and each other. Give Him praise always for whatever comes each day.

Jaime Naranjo:
We had marriage problems due to my drinking every day. We separated for four years and did not communicate with each other. We survived because we became Christians. We turned our lives and our marriage to the Lord. He is the one who turned everything around and made our relationship stronger, loyal and sincere.

SEXUAL RELATIONSHIP

Sexual Relationship

Fireworks to Chicken Noodle Soup

Chapter 7

My husband advised me against having this chapter in the book, as he felt it might make the participating couples feel uncomfortable writing about such a personal subject. I assured him that they were asked to write on any suggested topics that they wanted to expound on. For the most part, our parents didn't talk about this, so it is time that it was treated with dignity and given a voice that will help those reading this, in this unspoken adventure of life. I have saved this topic for the last in the book, as it is probably the most misunderstood and the hardest one to express feelings about.

Again, as I have said in several of the chapters, when you marry young, there is just a whole lot to learn about everything. I knew that he was a hunk and he thought I was a pretty hot chick! This is not a deep, intellectual discovery, but true for most couples in that attraction stage.... Fireworks and lots of emotions! Usually , men and women are wired different in this area of life also. By now, that news should not surprise you at all! Men are very visual in their romantic approach. Women tend to be very touch and talk oriented for their triggers toward romance. Men are stimulated by watching you wash dishes or cook...I'm not kidding! Women feel stimulated watching our husbands play with the kids, help in cleaning house, washing the dishes or taking time to walk on the beach and focus in conversation with us as their wives. Do you get the key words here: tender, helping, communicating! We want our man to be strong and a guys- guy, but we also want the tender side of him to be there . It is a tough role and shoes to fill.

One of the reasons that I saved this for the last chapter was quite apparent to me. All the previous subjects of finances, arguments, raising children, in-laws and crisis will profoundly affect what will be happening between the both of you romantically. Now you may think, if that is true, there is not going to be any sex for the rest of your marriage as one or more of those topics are usually happening at some time.

We have to understand that sex is the culmination of your emotions toward each other and also what is going on around you. I must say that men can take all exterior events and put them in a "little box" that never affects their present desires. On the other hand, a woman will always take *everything* that is happening and it will all be swirling around in her head at the same time. It will make her agitated that you can side-step the present "lurking" situation and be thinking about romance. The man will be in total disbelief that you are still thinking and pondering any distracting issues....why can't you just move on? Again , it is that difference of how we are made.

I want to suggest you Google this video by Mark Gungor, pastor, author, marriage seminar speaker, called: "Men's Brains, Women's Brains". I can't tell you how many times I have watched this video and laughed hysterically at how true this skit is on Men vs. Women in their thinking. It really should be required viewing by all young couples before marriage. But , if you have been married for awhile and are still confused about this person you are married to, this video will clear things up. We get to look at how differently we both approach all subjects and issues. I mention this video, so that each of you can understand why women get bogged down with the day-to-day and it affects the whole attitude for romance.

Moms have a very unique role in that it is our duty and in the Mother By-Laws to worry about all present and future events in our kids lives (Worrying puts a cloud over your intimate relationship with your husband.). Another video that will back this up is Anita Renfroe, author and Christian speaker's : "Momism's". I have personally seen this performed at a women's conference and was exhausted by the time she finished. She did this all in one breath and every bit of it was right on!! Woman really do dissect and over-analyze until we have completely exhausted our husbands, who may have thought that particular situation was "No big deal!"

Unfortunately , we have all learned about romance from outside sources that really didn't do us any favors in what we learned. It didn't get to the heart of what sex is all about: two people that are committed to each other through the thick and thin of it, through weight gains and hair losses, wrinkles that come from out of nowhere to tell us that time is moving on, holding tight as our kids move on with their lives, seeing jobs come and go and along with that so goes the money, watching us both go through different hair colors, making some moves from our favorite home of memories.....this is where you will get to the "Chicken Noodle Soup" stage. That stage where you are secure and feel the deep comfort that no one is going anywhere, regardless of what is going on around you. Your love/ romance is built on strength and courage ... not Fireworks and emotions. You stay the course because you have made a choice to be committed , loyal and trustworthy! There is nothing more beautiful than to just sometimes lye in bed and just hold each other. Your precious gift to each other is to lift each other in prayer that God will bless and watch over you . We need to have that covering of blessing from our spouses. When you have that, your romance can be a sweet kiss or a simple " I love you".

I will never forget when my parents told the five children that they were expecting a baby! What? Are you kidding me? I was in high school and my sister was in college. Mother and Dad were in their early 40's. I was in shock! First of all, why were they still having sex? Weren't five kids already a houseful? I really thought we were the Brady Bunch! How was I going to explain this to all my teenage friends? My Dad passed away from cancer when the youngest was two years old . He left my mom with a precious gift of a terrific son.

It taught me a lesson that sex will continue to be a vital part of every couples life forever. It just gets better, because you are secure in that persons love, no matter how your looks have changed over the years. You aren't really looking at the outside anymore because the inside has overtaken your "eyes". This is not to say that we don't need to look our best for our sweetie each day. Sometimes we just need to go get a makeover and a fresh new look. Throw out some of those old comfy clothes that a person on the street wouldn't wear! We can get a little too comfortable in this area.... ask a good friend what they would suggest you need to improve on. I have seen some transformations happen before that 10th Class Reunion. Some don't even go, because they have let themselves "go"! Pray and ask God to reveal to you how you can please your partner in physical and sexual ways. After all He did create this thing called sex, so I think we can certainly pray about it! He is the ultimate creative being, so I know He can help us to be *creative* and *fun* in this area.

Remember when life was fun and you laughed at the silliest things together….you may need to get back to that in some way. Maybe you have become such **a worrier**, that you are pretty much a grump all the time. Time to have a serious talk with the Lord and start letting Him take those worries. That is what it says in Philippians 4:4-7. We might be carrying a load that God intended to let Him carry for us. It is not easy, I *know* that from first-hand experience. That is how I know this verse by heart. I had to pray it over and over, because I was that person. I had to pray that God would change me from the inside out to be a loving and fun person again. And you know what….that is what He did for our marriage! He restored the love to forgive and give us fun back in the romance area of our life. To restore the trust, through some big hurdles that I had to overcome if we were going to start over.

Let me say, at this point, that if there has been an infidelity in your marriage….God tells us in the scriptures that He can "restore what the locusts have eaten". There have been many good marriages that this has happened to. Does it bring wreckage and ruin to your lives …Yes it will! But, I can tell you that with lots of prayer for the one that has wandered, God can do some mighty miracles to bring your marriage back together. God will help you start over, to build that trust and return a love to your hurting heart. It can be healed and your marriage can be better and stronger than it ever was , because it has been tested. You must realize, that Satan knows your weak areas and will work on those to destroy your marriage. That is why a prayer time with each other and for each other is your protective covering over your marriage. It is an on-going process that we can't take for granted. It may take some Christian marriage counseling to get to the bottom of how you both got to this point in your marriage. There are two sides to all problems, which is why it may take an unbiased 3rd person to help you sort through this.

Want to have some fun? Get some romantic music, some great massage oil and most of all a babysitter! The babysitter idea is one of most important. It is hard to disassociate a mom from her kids when they are in the next room and she is tense that they are going to open that door for "a drink of water"! That is a real mood downer. Couples can take turns sitting with each other kids to go out for a date night . The best foundation that you can give your kids is a loving home where mommy and daddy still kiss and love on each other….that gives them security that no matter what else is going on , there is a good home for them. Your "date night" should be a priority to get reconnected of why you got married in the first place. Remember, that one day the kids will be gone. You don't want to find yourself wondering who you are married to. It happens in the blink- of-an- eye! You get married , then comes the kids , then there goes the kids..... then there you are alone together. Let it be a wonderful time to enjoy life, that you can just go and do whatever, without worrying about the kids and where they are. It is that time in life that you have officially gone from *'Fireworks to Chicken Noodle Soup',* a place of comfort and security that reflect your years of being together ; it is a good place to be.

Women's Advice on Sexual Relationships

Pat Fryling:
Sex in a marriage is a beautiful thing, you feel so loved and so special, always making sure your spouse feels the same as you, which makes the desire more intimate and loving. Make sure you stay true to each other... thoughts and desires outside the marriage has no room in your life. Remember to take care of the garden, care for it and the beauty will flourish. Life is so busy today and time seems to steal way what is very precious to us and that is family and our time with each other. We always had a date night, sometimes it was just walking the mall or watching a movie, but it was our time together. It seems one cannot be without a cell phone or texting, just remember, it steals from your time together which you never can get back.

Debbie Morris:
This part of our marriage is so much more than sexual union. When you love your mate, you want to please them. Listen to your mate. If they have had an extra stressful time, be sensitive to that and loving towards them, whether you feel like it or not.

Sandra Dean:
Have fun! It's legal now. Your sex life is the best thermometer of the health of the marriage. God gave you different sex drives because He wants you to learn to put the other person first.

Gladys Myers:
Communication is the key to good relations. Be sensitive to each others needs/desires/moods. My Mother's advice was "love your husband"… you will have a much happier home life.

Be selective of your friends. Church friends very often become your life long supporters.

Don't let little disagreements grow – handle them in a Christian way.

Anonymous:
Talk to each other. This relationship will change as the years go on. Keep talking. Sometimes love means sex; sometimes it doesn't.

Mary Ann Martin:
We always make time for each other by going out for dinner or a movie for a date night. What is very intimate and special to me is to go to bed together and hold each other and talk about the day. He is showing me that he cares about my day and what is going on with my life. Talking is a woman's love language.

Kay Carol Pemberton:
Sex is a vital part of a healthy marriage. Women tend to tire and sometimes be less interested. Women must understand the needs of the husbands. Discussion about sexual needs will help a marriage remain strong.

Netta White:
Show your love and affection for one another, e.g. a hug every morning and evening, whenever! A phone call, just to see how his day is going. You're letting him know that you're thinking of him. Having sex with your husband is the culmination of the flirtation that's been going on throughout the day – it is the glue that keeps your marriage strong. "Make each other happy."

Sylvia Hankin:
Sexual relations between married couples should always be special. It is not sex, but lovemaking. Anyone can have sex. But, when shared between a man and a woman, who are married, who become one during lovemaking, now there is nothing more special than that. Try to make time for each other.

Vicki Clinton:
As a wife and husband you are committed to fulfilling each other. Be sensitive to each other. Sex is a way God has enabled for a husband and wife to come together, without holding back, to be completely naked, both mentally and physically. This nakedness brings about a love and trust that you will not have with anyone else.

Phyllis Haas:
There should be no other except between husband and wife.
Read : I Corinthians 6:19-20.

Vicky Abney:
Oh, to be young again! Hopefully, you are on the same page in this category. Have conversations, be honest. Make it special. Keep a sense of humor and always let your husband know he is the best thing you could ever possibly have. Don't allow anyone to make your spouse feel more special than you do. It's SUPER important to guys!! It's their love language.

Men's Advice on Sexual Relationship

Ron White:
This is bonding time with your spouse. Sex is the expression of love you have for each other. Don't use sex as a weapon – it's not going to work! It causes anger, frustration, suspicion and fights, which sometimes can lead to infidelity. "Make each other happy."

Larry Pemberton:
Men need to know their wives and understand their needs and desires. Healthy sexual activity is a married couple's way of showing their love for each other. It should continue to be a vital part of the marriage for many years.

E. Don Myers:
We have asked God for direction in work, illness, church life and felt his guidance. When Gladys and I married in 1949, our parents and grandparents had been married for years. No divorces in either family. We had the same goals, buy a home, educate our son when he became college age and have some savings.

God blessed our efforts. Has not been smooth road but God has always been there for us. REMAIN SWEETHEARTS!!!

Fred Akin:

This will get better with time. You have to ask/communicate what the other needs.

It is an on going learning process. Loving your mate makes the sex better. If there are other major issues affecting the couple, then the sexual relation will usually suffer. Women control 100% of the sexual relationship.

Ade Fryling:

The sexual drive and the hunger drive are our two strongest drives. The hunger drive is a necessity as it is the bodies way to inform us of it's need for food. The hunger drive can be influenced by smells, sounds, tastes or touch. The pleasure experienced by the taste, smell, sweetness or savor of foods arouses eating even if hunger is not there. The sex drive is similar. Sex was created in man as the means to propagate the species. Both the sex and hunger drive varies in individuals. Conditions in life, age, stress and wellness modifies the urgings toward the need. As hunger can be influenced by the senses, so can the urge of sex. This is the reason God demands sex after marriage only. Pre-martial sex with various partners will provide a comparison, when marriage happens that complicates the intimacy in a marriage. Sex can happen mechanically, and certainly without love. This experience can be compared to sex as it exists in the animal world. Some species share a mate for life, and there is visible affection in evidence, but the sexual intimacy produced with love is beyond any other experience. That is why God instructed couples to leave family ties, and that the two individuals should become one flesh. That is also why it is absolutely necessary to be faithful in the marriage relationship, as joining to another individual would destroy the one flesh requirement. Sex in marriage is always expressed in fulfillment of the marriage partner, being sensitive to each ones needs or desires. Insensitivity in sex can damage the relationship and dampen the deepness of love between the couple. Make time for each other to respond to sex through love.

Harry Reese

God created sex and Solomon (the wisest man on earth) wrote about it. This is the time spent unraveling the mysteries of the other person and knowing them in a way that is unique to the relationship and only you know.

Louis Ikerd

Men and women need to understand that this is the ultimate way of saying I love you. Men need to know that their wives are not a sex toy and women need to understand that sex is not a bargaining chip for something that they want. Respect, understanding and patience needs to be exhibited by both partners in this area.

Mike Sullivan:

Another important factor in a successful marriage is the sexual relationship. It is amazing how it can deteriorate after marriage if not nurtured by both parties. We should make efforts to maintain our looks. Give encouraging comments, occasional touches, intimate words. Each partner should be very much aware of the desires of the other. Our concern for our partner should equal or exceed our concern for ourselves.

Terry D. Hankin

This is an intimate subject that be should be just that – intimate, between a married couple who love each other. If you truly love each other you will try to make it as special as possible for each other. Keep your love true to each other only.

YOUR DECISION

Your Decision

"Choose This Day Whom You Will Serve"

Chapter 8

I hope you have enjoyed our 'little chat' about life and what it will take to have a successful marriage. All the couples and I have shared our lives, in hopes that you will one day be in the *'25 Plus Club'*. As you can see, it is for the strong and courageous, that will persevere through the challenges of life. You may be saying "I don't know if I can do it", "It's just too hard", "Where did they find such strength and courage?"

All of this is great counseling and advice, but it all starts with the heart and your mind. I want to take this time to share with you how to become a Christian , which is the foundation of all our lives. We come from different backgrounds and churches, but we serve the same God . He alone can give you courage and strength to face whatever comes into your life. He wants to give you an abundant life with meaning and purpose if you will only trust Him.

What can you do to become a Christian?

1. Recognize that God loves you completely and wants the best for your life.

John 3:16- "For God so loved the world(you), that He gave His only begotten Son, that whosoever believes in Him should not perish but have everlasting life".

2. Recognize that you need help in this life.

Romans 3:23- "For all have sinned and come short of the glory of God."

3. Recognize that God has made a way to get that help.

Romans 6:23- "For the wages of sin is death, but the **gift** of God is eternal life through Jesus Christ, our Lord".

4. Recognize that He wants all to come to know Him.

Romans 10:13- "Whoever calls on the name of the Lord will be saved".

Coming to know Jesus Christ as your Lord and Savior, is a simple act of trusting Him with all the decisions in your life and that He is who you go to in prayer about everything. You now want His direction and counsel about everything in your life. After all, He created you and He certainly knows what is the best for you in all situations.

So where do you go from here?

God wants you to be in a church family that can nurture you and help you to grow in this new walk; "Forsake not the assembling of yourselves together". Seek out and pray about where God wants you to get planted. Churches are made up of other families like yours that are in a process of growing and learning. It may take some time to find the right church, one that honors God, preaches the Bible and Jesus Christ from the pulpit, active ministries, good teaching classes for all ages and a loving fellowship. These are the right ingredients to look for. Pray and ask God to show you where that is and I promise you, He will guide your steps. There may be a process of visiting several churches, but God will give you and your family a peace that you are in the right place.

Keep in mind that I did not say find a perfect church as there is no such thing.....we are all sinners saved by grace and we will not be perfect until we reach heaven. But we are all in a process of growing in the Lord on a daily basis. There will be times that every one of us will stumble and fall. But God picks us up and dust us off and forgives us by the blood of Jesus Christ to wipe the slate clean that gets us back on track : 1 John 1:9. He is teaching us to rely on the power of the Holy Spirit that will empower us to walk daily with Him…not in our power but in His!

Some daily personal spiritual growth exercises :

1. Get a Bible and read something each day…feed your spiritual soul!

Psalm 119:11- " Your Word have I hidden in my heart that I might not sin against you".

Hebrews 4:12-"For the word of God is living and powerful, and sharper than any two-edged sword, piercing even to the division of soul and spirit, and of joints and marrow, and is a discerner of the thoughts and intents of the heart".

Psalm 119:103-105 Luke 21:33 Matthew 4:4 1 Peter 1:23-25 John 6:63

2. Pray each day and ask God to guide and direct your path. Bring your requests and lay them at His feet.

Philippians 4:6-7-" Be anxious for nothing. But in prayer and supplication let your request be made known unto God. And the peace of God which passes all understanding will keep your hearts and your minds in Christ Jesus".

Jeremiah 33:3- "Call to Me, and I will answer you , and show you great and mighty things, which you do not know".

Matthew 18:18-19 James5:16-18 Luke 11:9 Matthew 6:5-6 Psalms55:17

3. You will want to share your new faith with others in a loving way.

Matthew 5:14-16- "You are the light of the world. A city that is set on a hill cannot be hidden. Nor do they light a lamp and put it under a basket, but on a lampstand, and it gives light to all who are in the house. Let your light so shine before men, that they may see your good works and glorify your Father in heaven".

Luke 11:33 Ephesians 6:18-20 1 Peter 3:8-11
1 Peter 3:15

4.Support your local church with your time, talents and finances.

Luke 6: 38- "Give and it will be given unto you: good measure, pressed down, shaken together, and running over will be put into your bosom. For with the same measure that you use it, it will be measured back to you".

2 Corinthians 9:6-7 Luke 16:10-11 Proverbs 22:9
2 Chronicles 31:5

5.Grow in your faith by walking with Him daily.

1 Peter 1:7-9-"That the genuineness of your faith, being much more precious than gold that perishes, though it is tested by fire, may be found to praise, honor and glory at the revelation of Jesus Christ, whom having not seen you love. Though now you do not see Him, yet believing, you rejoice with joy inexpressible and full of the glory, receiving the end of your faith – the salvation of your souls".

Colossians 3:16 1 John 2:3-6 John 15:4-7 1 John 2:28 Proverbs8:34

Conclusion:

I pray that this book has enriched and been a blessing to your life. May your heart and your home be changed by the advice and wisdom that has been shared by all the couples that freely gave of their time and talents.

Numbers 6: 24-26- " May the Lord bless and protect you; may the Lord's face radiate with joy because of you; may He be gracious to you , show you His favor and give you His peace". Amen and Amen.

Thank You

There are so many people that have helped in getting this book written. I asked four couples , from the start of day one, to be my *Advisor Council* , to be in prayer for me as I wrote this: Mike and Barbara Sullivan, Patti and Harry Reese, Dempsie and Vicki Clinton, and Louis and Mary Ann Martin. These couples know Fred and I from start to finish, and have loved us through the thick and thin times of life. These are the people that you can call at 2:00am for help and they will be there. Barbara , Patti and Vicki are my sisters and Mary Ann is my 'adopted' sister.

My *Senior Advisor* is Frances Knight, whom I have gone to the same church with for twenty-seven years. She is a Bible study teacher for the Ladies Class for 40 years and has authored a book on "Prayer". She has been invaluable in her knowledge of "what to do next". You have to know, that when God placed in my heart to write a book, I was clueless of what to do. He has put people in my path at every turn to get this done..... Amazing...Jehovah Jireh!!!

My sister, Vicki, volunteered to do a lot of the typing which was huge. Again, I don't type. Isn't that hilarious! God asked me to write a book and I don't type. So that part is a real labor of love for me to do. Thank you , Vicki for helping with the comments part of the book.

Frances Knight and Mary Anne Betancourt helped in critiquing the book...to make it the best that it could be. A big job that they both volunteered to do for me. Again, for every step, God put help in my path to get this done.

I also asked my precious girlfriends to be my *Prayer Partners*. I would send out an email that I might need special prayer for a part of the book that had me stumped. What a blessing to know that I could count on them to be genuinely concerned and would lift me in prayer. Girlfriends are a gift from God…cherish them: Christian(daughter), Matilde(daughter-in-law)), Carol, Cathy, Julia, Gloria, Janet, Jeni, Tracy, Jodie, Judy, Karen, Melissa, Nancy, Peggy, Rayne, Sheyenne, Shirley, Suzanne, Laurie, Mary Anne .

The next group were my *Anchor Partners*. I asked these people to find couples in their circles of friendships that would fit the qualifications needed for the book.:

Barbara Sullivan, Carol Johnson, Patti Reese, Mary Anne Betancourt and Bernard Cleghorn. I needed their help in finding couples across Texas that would participate. I would not have a book if they had not graciously volunteered to help with this huge task.

Acknowledgments

Let me introduce the couples that are in this book. They graciously volunteered to take the time to pour their hearts out so that other couples would learn from their years of wisdom. How do I say *"Thank You"* adequately for their help? I don't know some of these couples, except that they are my brothers and sisters in the Lord and have withstood the test of time to be in the '**25 Plus Club**':

1. **Mike and Barbara Sullivan-Pastor**
Married 38 years
Spirit of Praise Church Harlingen, TX

2. **Dempsie and Vicki Clinton**
Married 39 years
First Baptist Church Rio Hondo,TX

3. **Harry and Patti Reese**
Married 30 years
The Village Church/Northway Dallas, TX

4. **Louis and Mary Ann Martin**
Married 36 years
First Baptist Church Rio Hondo, TX

5. **Lionel and Mary Anne Betancourt**
Married 49 years
First Baptist Church Harlingen,TX

6.Bob and Frances Knight
Married 57 years
First Baptist Church Rio Hondo, TX

7.Duane and Jodie Stryker
Married 28 years
First Baptist Church Harlingen, TX

8.Larry and Kay Carol Pemberton
Married 27 years
Village Church/Northway Dallas, Tx

9.Adrian and Patricia Fryling
Married 55 years
Winter Texans at First Baptist Church Harlingen, TX

10.Ron and Netta White
Married 38 years
St. Helena's Episcopal Church Boerne, Tx

11.Jaime and Elma Naranjo
Married 43 years
First Baptist Church Rio Hondo, TX

12.Louis and Diana L. Ikerd
Married 32 years
First Baptist Church Harlingen, TX

13. Paul and Vicky Abney
Married 32 years
Austin Ridge Bible Church Austin, TX

14.Ralph and Lea Cochran
Married 45 years
First Baptist Church Rio Hondo, TX

15. Don and Gladys Myers
Married 61 years
The Village Church/Northway Dallas, TX

16.J.B. and Debbie Morris
Married 30 years
Georgetown Baptist Church Pottsboro, TX

17.Laurel and Phyllis Haas
Married 54 years
First Baptist Church Rio Hondo, TX

18.James and Sandra Dean
Married 30 years
Sherman Bible Church Sherman, TX

19.Terry and Sylvia Hankin
Married 28 years
Spirit of Praise Church Harlingen, TX

20. Fred and Joyce Akin-Author
Married 45 years
First Baptist Church Rio Hondo, TX

Other Suggested Books:

1. Sacred Marriage-Gary Thomas

2. Men are From Mars,Women from Venus- John Gray

3. The Five Love Languages – Gary Chapman

4. Hidden Keys of a Loving, Lasting Marriage – Gary Smalley

5. Romantic Lovers – David and Carole Hocking

6. The Act of Marriage – Tim and Beverly LaHaye

7. The Act of Marriage Over 40 – Tim and Beverly LaHaye

8. Quiet Time for Couples – H. Norman Wright

9. His Needs, Her Needs – Willard F. Harley ,Jr.

10. The Love Dare – Stephen Kendrick
    Fireproof(book from the Christian movie)

11. Love and Respect: The Love She Most Desires, The Respect He
    Desperately Need –Dr. Emerson Eggerich(Focus on the Family)

12. Everybody Wins: The Chapman Guide to Solving Conflict
    Without Arguing – Gary Chapman

13. Dare to Discipline:The New Strong-Willed Child –
Dr. James Dobson

14. Money and Marriage God's Way – Howard Dayton

15. Financial Peace: More Than Enough – Dave Ramsey

16. Master Your Money – Ron Blue

17. Debt Proof Your Marriage – Mary Hunt

18. Debt Free Living: The Word on Finances – Suze Orman

19. The Purpose Driven Life – Rick Warren

20. Forgive and Forget : Healing the Hurts We Don't Deserve-
Lewis B. Smeades

21. Your Best Life Now – Joel Osteen

22. Christianity Alive! With Prayer Power – Frances Knight(new)

23. The Holy Bible- Your preferred version
#1 Best Seller